DISASTERS!

**21 Famous Disasters—
With Exercises for Developing
Critical Reading Skills**

Dan Dramer

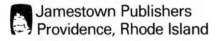 Jamestown Publishers
Providence, Rhode Island

SECOND EDITION

DISASTERS!
Second Edition

21 Famous Disasters—With Exercises
for Developing Critical Reading Skills

Catalog No. 768
©1982, 1995 by Jamestown Publishers

Cover and Text Design by Thomas Ewing Malloy, based
on an original design by Deborah Hulsey Christie

Printed in the United States of America

1 2 3 4 5 6 7 8 HS 99 98 97 96 95

ISBN 0-89061-766-X

Contents

To the Teacher

INTRODUCTION

Disasters are one of our main topics of conversation. They fill a major portion of the daily news, and they are often featured by the publishing, movie, and television industries. Even in the earliest historical records there is mention of shipwrecks, floods, famines, and other such misfortunes. Disasters can be so tragic and compelling that you never forget them. In *Disasters!*, Second Edition, you'll find some of the world's best-known tragedies. Your students will find them fascinating.

   Disasters! provides subject matter for thoughtful interpretation and discussion, while challenging your students in four critical reading categories: main idea, important details, inferences, and vocabulary in context. *Disasters!* can also help your students improve their reading rates. Timing of the selections is optional, but many teachers find it an effective motivating device.

   Disasters! consists of twenty-one units divided into three groups of seven units each. All the stories in a group are on the same reading level. Group One is at the sixth-grade reading level, Group Two at the seventh, and Group Three at the eighth, as assessed by the Fry Formula for Estimating Readability.

HOW TO USE THIS BOOK

Introducing the Book. This text, used creatively, can be an effective tool for learning certain critical reading skills. We suggest that you begin by introducing the students to the contents and format of the book. Examine the book with the students to see how it is set up and what it is about. Discuss the title. Ask your students to name some recent great disasters. Read through the table of contents as a class to gain an overview of the disasters that will be encountered.

The Sample Unit. To learn what is contained in each unit and how to proceed through a unit, turn to the Sample Unit on pages 10–15. After you have examined these pages yourself, work through the Sample Unit with your students so that they may have a clear understanding of the purpose of the book and of how they are to use it.

The Sample Unit is set up exactly as the regular units are. At the beginning there is a photograph or illustration accompanied by a caption. The story is next, followed by four types of comprehension exercises: Finding the Main Idea, Recalling Facts, Making Inferences, and Using Words Precisely.

Begin by having someone in the class read aloud the caption that appears with the picture. Then give the students a few moments to study the picture. Ask for their thoughts on what the story will be about. Continue the discussion for a minute or so. Then have the students read the story. (You may wish to time the students' reading in order to help them improve their reading speed as well as their comprehension. A Words-per-Minute table is located in the back of the book to help the students figure their reading rates.)

Then go through the sample questions as a class. An explanation of the comprehension skill and directions for answering the questions are given at the beginning of each exercise. Make sure all the students understand how to figure their scores. The correct answers and sample scores are filled in. Explanations of all the correct answers are also given within the sample Main Idea and Making Inferences exercises to help the students understand how to think through these question types.

As the students are working their way through the Sample Unit, be sure to have them turn to the Words-per-Minute table on pages 154 and 155 (if you have timed their reading) and the Reading Speed and Critical Reading Scores graphs on pages 156 and 157 at the appropriate points. Explain to the students the purpose of each, and read the directions with them. Be sure they understand how the table and graphs will be used. You will probably have to help them find and mark their scores for the first unit or two.

Timing the Story. If you are going to time your students' reading, explain to them your reason for doing so: to help them keep track of and improve their reading rates.

Here's one way of timing. Have all the students in the class begin reading the story at the same time. After one minute has passed, write on the chalkboard the time that has elapsed, and begin updating it at ten-second intervals (1:00, 1:10, 1:20, etc.). Tell the students to copy down the last time shown on the chalkboard when they have finished reading. They should write their reading time in the space designated after the story.

Have the students check their reading rates by using the Words-per-Minute table on pages 154 and 155. They should then enter their reading speed on the Reading Speed graph on page 156. Graphing their reading rates allows the students to keep track of improvement in their reading speed.

Working Through Each Unit. If the students have carefully completed all parts of the Sample Unit, they should be ready to tackle the regular units. In each unit, begin by having the students look at the illustration or photograph. Then have someone in the class read aloud the caption, just as you did in the Sample Unit. Discuss the topic of the story, and allow the students time to study the illustration again.

Then have the students read the story. If you are timing them, have the students enter their reading time, find their reading speed, and record their speed on the graph after they have finished reading the story.

Next, direct the students to complete the four comprehension exercises *without* looking back at the story. When they have finished, go over the questions and answers with them. The students will grade their own answers and make the necessary corrections. They should then enter Critical Reading Scores on the graph on page 157.

The Graphs. Students enjoy graphing their work. Graphs show, in a concrete and easily understandable way, how a student is progressing. Seeing a line of progressively rising scores gives students the incentive to continue to strive for improvement.

Check the graphs regularly. This will allow you to establish a routine for reviewing each student's progress. Discuss with each student what the graphs show and what kind of progress you expect. Establish guidelines and warning signals so that students will know when to approach you for counseling and advice.

RELATED TEXTS

If you find that your students enjoy and benefit from the stories and skills exercises in *Disasters!,* you may be interested in *Phenomena, Monsters, Heroes, Eccentrics, Apparitions, Calamities,* and *Aliens & UFOs,* seven related Jamestown texts. All feature high-interest stories and work in four critical reading comprehension skills. As in *Disasters!,* the units in those books are divided into three groups, at reading levels six, seven, and eight.

SAMPLE UNIT

*The news from the **Andrea Doria** that July night was unbelievable. Not since the **Titanic** disaster in 1912 had there been such a horrible accident at sea. But would the Italian luxury liner sink? The truth was captured on film the next morning. In this award-winning photograph, the **Andrea Doria** slips below the surface 11 hours after colliding with the **Stockholm**.*

Andrea Doria Buried at Sea

It was a warm July evening in 1956. The *Andrea Doria,* after six days at sea, was nearing the end of its voyage to New York City from Genoa, Italy. The Italian liner carried a crew of 575 and 1,134 passengers. Movie stars, the mayor of Philadelphia, businessmen, and poor Italian families were among those on board the giant vessel. No other passenger ship excelled the *Andrea Doria* in luxury.

In a dense fog, the *Andrea Doria* sailed at top speed toward the United States mainland, about 100 miles away. It had entered an area of the Atlantic Ocean known as "Times Square," so named because ship traffic there is usually heavy.

One of the ships in Times Square that night was the *Stockholm,* a sleek, modern Swedish passenger ship. The *Stockholm* had departed from New York and was bound for its home port.

Around 11:00 P.M. an Italian boy stood on the *Andrea Doria*'s deck, peering through the fog. He tried to catch sight of land. He knew that Nantucket, an island off the coast of Massachusetts, was out there somewhere in the pea soup fog. He strained his eyes searching through the muck. Suddenly, he thought he saw something. It took a few more seconds for him to realize what it was. He saw the enormous bulk of the *Stockholm*—and the great edge of the white bow was heading straight for him!

Other people saw the *Stockholm* too. The captain and crew of the *Andrea Doria* had been watching the Swedish liner for some time on the radar screen. Captain Piero Calamai, a veteran sailor, thought that if the two ships held their course they would pass safely starboard to starboard. It wasn't until he saw the *Stockholm*'s lights that he realized the extreme danger he faced. He tried to steer his ship away from the *Stockholm,* but there wasn't enough time. The *Stockholm* started to turn to avoid a collision, then for some reason it suddenly turned again. Calamai drew back from the railing as the two ships rushed toward each other. Seconds later the *Stockholm* crashed into *Andrea Doria*'s side. The Italian liner shook from end to end and briefly lifted out of the water.

The *Stockholm* had a razor-sharp bow designed especially for breaking through ice. Now, that icebreaker bow sliced a V-shaped gash through the *Andrea Doria.* It finally came to a stop 30 feet inside the stricken ship. When the *Stockholm* reversed its engines and pulled back, the sea poured into the jagged, 40-foot hole in the side of the Italian ship. The *Andrea Doria* had received its death blow.

About 40 passengers aboard the *Andrea Doria* were killed instantly in their cabins or drowned. Walter Carlin, from Brooklyn, New York, was brushing his teeth in his cabin. The impact knocked him to the bathroom floor. Dazed and bruised, he walked back to the bedroom and found the *Stockholm*'s bow inside his cabin. His wife, who had been sleeping in her bunk, was dead. Carlin stood stunned as the ship's bow slowly moved backward. To his horror, it pulled his wife's bunk along with it. His wife's body slipped quickly into the sea.

Fourteen-year-old Linda Morgan was asleep in an upper bunk in cabin 52. Her younger sister slept in the lower bunk. After the collision there was nothing left of their cabin and the girls had disappeared. A crewman on the *Stockholm* found Linda, alive, lying in the wreckage. By some miracle, Linda survived being thrown from her bed and into the *Stockholm*'s bow. Her sister, however, was killed.

Passengers on the upper deck of the *Andrea Doria* were unaware of the chaos below. Cabins on five levels were completely destroyed. Thick smoke, twisted metal, and water filled the hallways. Fuel tanks had ruptured and were spraying oil. Severely injured people trapped under the wreckage were screaming. Others rushed to the stairways and pushed and shoved their way to the upper deck. Their clothes were wet and torn, and they were covered with oil and blood.

Aboard the *Stockholm* there was little panic and only a few casualties. The ship's bow was torn and bent like a discarded tin can, but the liner was able to stay afloat. Through the fog, passengers on the Swedish ship could hear the cries coming from the *Andrea Doria*.

Listing to one side, the damaged Italian ship was now in serious danger. Captain Calamai ordered the lifeboats lowered, but because of the list some boats were useless. Passengers panicked and started fighting for a place on the boats. The captain sent out an SOS. Four ships in the area answered the signal. Meanwhile, the *Stockholm* sent over its lifeboats and rescued 545 people.

A small freighter, the *Cape Ann,* arrived soon after the crash and picked up 129 passengers from the *Andrea Doria.* The *William H. Thomas,* steaming hard to the scene, picked up 150 victims. Another ship, the *Allen,* saved 77 people.

A large French liner, the *Ile de France,* was on its way to Europe when it heard the SOS. The captain radioed his message and then ordered the ships lights turned on. The vessel had a panel of electric lights on each side of its hull that spelled out the ship's name. Passengers on the *Andrea Doria* could see the name of the French ship far in the distance and knew that more help was on the way. The *Ile de France* sailed at full speed and arrived in two hours. It rescued about 750 survivors and carried them to New York City.

The badly wounded *Andrea Doria* managed to stay afloat for 11 hours after the crash. That was long enough for all the survivors to be rescued. The final death count was 51.

Just after 10:00 in the morning the *Andrea Doria* slipped below the ocean, bow first, and sank in 225 feet of water.

An investigation of the accident tried to determine if either ship had been at fault. The fog had been especially thick that July night. The *Andrea Doria* and the *Stockholm* had been in the busiest part of the Atlantic. They were headed in opposite directions in a lane used for shipping. Usually a ship stays to one side of the shipping lane. The *Stockholm* was not on the side of the lane generally used by Europe-bound ships. Both ships, however, had radar equipment in working order. How could the ships not have seen each other in plenty of time to change course? There were many theories, but nobody has ever found the answer. ∎

If you have been timed while reading this selection, enter your reading time below. Then turn to the Words-per-Minute table on page 154 and look up your reading speed (words per minute). When you are working through the regular units, you will then enter your reading speed on the graph on page 156.

READING TIME: Sample Unit

_____ : _____
Minutes   Seconds

The Andrea Doria *leaves behind a whirlpool of debris after sinking to its grave.*

How well did you read?

- *The four types of questions that follow appear in each unit in this book. The directions for each type of question tell you how to mark your answers. In the Sample Unit, the answers are marked for you. Also, for the Main Idea and Making Inferences exercises, explanations of the answers are given, to help you understand how to think through these question types. Read through these exercises carefully.*

- *When you have finished all four exercises in a unit, you will check your work by using the answer key that starts on page 150. For each right answer, you will put a check mark (✓) on the line beside the box. For each wrong answer, you will write the correct answer on the line.*

- *For scoring each exercise, you will follow the directions below the questions. In this unit, sample scores are entered as examples.*

A FINDING THE MAIN IDEA

Look at the three statements below. One expresses the main idea of the story you just read. A good main idea statement answers two questions: it tells *who* or *what* is the subject of the story, and it answers the understood question *does what?* or *is what?* Another statement is *too broad;* it is vague and doesn't tell much about the topic of the story. The third statement is *too narrow;* it tells about only one part of the story.

Match the statements with the three answer choices below by writing the letter of each answer in the box in front of the statement it goes with.

M—Main Idea   **B—Too Broad**   **N—Too Narrow**

✓   N 1. The *Stockholm* cut a 40-foot hole in the *Andrea Doria's* side.
[This statement is true, but it is *too narrow*. It gives only one piece, or detail, from the story.]

✓   B 2. When large ships collide, there can be considerable damage.
[This statement is true, but it is *too broad*. The story is about what happened to the *Andrea Doria* and the *Stockholm*.]

✓   M 3. The *Andrea Doria* received its death blow after colliding with the *Stockholm* in a dense fog.
[This statement is the *main idea*. It tells you what the reading selection is about—two ships colliding at sea. It also tells you that there was dense fog.]

15 Score 15 points for a correct *M* answer
10 Score 5 points for each correct *B* or *N* answer
25 TOTAL SCORE: Finding the Main Idea

B RECALLING FACTS

How well do you remember the facts in the story you just read? Put an x in the box in front of the correct answer to each of the multiple-choice questions below.

1. The point in the Atlantic where the ships collided was
   ✓ [x] a. heavily traveled.
   ___ [ ] b. deserted because of the fog.
   ___ [ ] c. not used by luxury liners.

2. The *Stockholm*
   ___ [ ] a. was badly damaged by the crash.
   ___ [ ] b. sank after the crash.
   ✓ [x] c. crushed its bow in the crash.

3. Most of the *Andrea Doria* passengers
   ___ [ ] a. died instantly.
   ✓ [x] b. were rescued by the *Ile de France.*
   ___ [ ] c. were picked up by the *Stockholm.*

4. The *Stockholm* caused so much damage to the *Andrea Doria* because it
   ✓ [x] a. had an ice-cutter bow.
   ___ [ ] b. was sailing at full speed.
   ___ [ ] c. was made of very hard steel.

5. The *Andrea Doria* stayed afloat for
   ___ [ ] a. 24 hours.
   ___ [ ] b. 15 hours.
   ✓ [x] c. 11 hours.

Score 5 points for each correct answer

__25__ TOTAL SCORE: Recalling Facts

C MAKING INFERENCES

An inference is a judgment that is made or an idea that is arrived at based on facts or on information that is given. You make an inference when you understand something that is *not* stated directly but that is *implied,* or suggested, by the facts that are given.

Below are five statements that are judgments or ideas that have been arrived at from the facts of the story. Write the letter *C* in the box in front of each statement that is a correct inference. Write the letter *F* in front of each faulty inference.

C—Correct Inference   F—Faulty Inference

✓ [F] 1. Passengers aboard the *Stockholm* feared that their ship would sink.
[This is a *faulty* inference. There is nothing in the story to suggest that the *Stockholm* was in danger of sinking.]

✓ [F] 2. Captain Calamai warned his passengers to prepare for a crash.
[This is a *faulty* inference. The story does not mention that the captain talked to the passengers before the crash.]

✓ [C] 3. The ships might have avoided a collision if it had been a clear night.
[This is a *correct* inference. The story says that there was thick fog.]

✓ [C] 4. At first, passengers on the upper deck of the *Andrea Doria* did not think the damage was serious.
[This is a *correct* inference. The passengers realized later what had happened on the decks below.]

✓ [F] 5. The *Stockholm* did not participate in the rescue effort.
[This is a *faulty* inference. The story says that the *Stockholm* sent lifeboats over to the damaged ship.]

Score 5 points for each correct answer

__25__ TOTAL SCORE: Making Inferences

D USING WORDS PRECISELY

Each of the numbered sentences below contains an underlined word or phrase from the story you have just read. Under the sentence are three definitions. One is a *synonym,* a word that means the same or almost the same thing: *big* and *large.* One is an *antonym,* a word that has the opposite or nearly opposite meaning: *love* and *hate.* One is an unrelated word; it has a completely *different* meaning. Match the definitions with the three answer choices by writing the letter that stands for each answer in the box in front of the definition it goes with.

S—Synonym   A—Antonym   D—Different

1. No other passenger ship underlined(excelled) the *Andrea Doria* in luxury.

✓ S a. was superior to

✓ A b. was worse than

✓ D c. was worth more

2. He saw the enormous bulk of the *Stockholm.* . . .

✓ A a. small section

✓ S b. main body

✓ D c. fiber

3. Captain Piero Calamai, a veteran sailor, thought that if the two ships held their course they would pass safely. . . .

✓ D a. former

✓ A b. unskilled

✓ S c. experienced

4. It [the bow] finally came to a stop 30 feet inside the stricken ship.

✓ D a. filled with sorrow

✓ S b. damaged

✓ A c. untouched

5. Fuel tanks had ruptured and were spraying oil.

✓ S a. cracked

✓ D b. separated

✓ A c. sealed

15 Score 3 points for each correct *S* answer
10 Score 1 point for each correct *A* or *D* answer
25 TOTAL SCORE: Using Words Precisely

● *Enter the four total scores in the spaces below, and add them together to find your Critical Reading Score. Then record your Critical Reading Score on the graph on page 157.*

_____	Finding the Main Idea
_____	Recalling Facts
_____	Making Inferences
_____	Using Words Precisely
_____	CRITICAL READING SCORE: Sample Unit

To the Student

People find disasters of any kind fascinating. Since early times, stories of earthquakes, floods, famines, plagues, and other misfortunes have been passed down by word of mouth or recorded in diaries or journals. These tragic stories have become an important and interesting part of history. Today, we have many books, movies, and TV shows about similar terrible events. *Disasters!* brings you the stories of twenty-one of the world's best-known disasters.

While you are enjoying these compelling stories, you will be developing your reading skills. This book assumes that you already are a fairly good reader. *Disasters!* is for students who want to read faster and to increase their understanding of what they read. If you complete all twenty-one units—reading the stories and completing the exercises—you will surely improve both your reading rate and your comprehension.

GROUP ONE

What happened to Avianca Flight 52? On a cold January evening residents of Glen Cove, New York, were asking this very question. The plane had just dropped from the sky and crashed in their neighborhood. As residents raced to the crash site, they heard the moans and cries of wounded passengers. When investigators arrived and sifted through the wreckage, they expected to find some answers. Unfortunately, there were few to be found.

Emergency on Avianca Flight 52

Passengers on Avianca Flight 52 breathed a sigh of relief as the lights of New York City came into view. It had been a long flight from Colombia, South America. Several delays had made it even longer. But the tension eased now that they were over Glen Cove, New York, a suburb 15 miles northeast of the big city. Soon they would arrive at John F. Kennedy International Airport, their final destination. The 154 passengers had no idea that their lives were in danger.

In the cockpit, Avianca's pilot, copilot, and flight engineer were frantic. The fuel gauges showed dangerously low levels. The old plane—if there were no further trouble—had just enough fuel to land at Kennedy Airport. Because of bad weather in New York, Flight 52 had been delayed a quarter of an hour over Norfolk, Virginia, and a half hour over New Jersey. Now it had been circling Kennedy Airport for three-quarters of an hour. All that circling had wasted precious fuel.

The crew of Flight 52 were all experienced flyers. They had worked for Avianca, the national airline of Colombia, for a long time and knew about the problems. The airline had the second worst safety record in the world and a history of transporting drugs. Smugglers constantly used the airline to carry cocaine from Colombia to the United States. Since 1986 American customs agents had seized more than 5,000 pounds of cocaine from 14 Avianca flights. But on January 25, 1990, there was only one thing on the minds of the flight crew. It was fuel.

Air traffic controllers at Kennedy Airport were having their own share of trouble that night. Thick fog and wind sheers gusting across the runways were making landings hazardous. The tower had to redirect most incoming flights to Boston, where the weather was better.

About 8:45 P.M. Avianca's Captain Laureano Cavides told his copilot to inform the control tower that Flight 52 did not have enough fuel to fly to Boston. The crew had known for an hour that the fuel was seriously low but had kept the information quiet. When copilot Mauricio Klotz finally radioed the tower, his message in Spanish was brief. In a calm and confident voice, he told the control tower that Flight 52 needed a priority landing because of low fuel. Unfortunately, he never once used the word *emergency* in either Spanish or English. The tower asked them to circle in a holding pattern for five minutes. As they waited, Captain Cavides kept asking Klotz, "Did you tell Kennedy we have a fuel emergency?" The copilot assured the captain that the tower understood their problem and would clear them to land. But the control tower did *not* understand just how critical Flight 52's fuel problem really was. And the

situation worsened when another controller took over monitoring the flight. He had no idea that the Avianca plane was practically running on fumes.

Meanwhile, Captain Cavides was yelling in the cockpit. He couldn't hear, for some reason, what his copilot was saying. The cockpit voice recorder later revealed that Cavides said again and again, "Tell me things louder because I'm not hearing it."

Finally, Avianca was cleared to land. Captain Cavides brought the plane down but missed his first attempt at Kennedy because of high winds and low clouds. The missed landing and abrupt climb of the plane used up more precious fuel. The pilot told the tower he would bring Flight 52 around for another approach. This time Cavides instructed the copilot in no uncertain terms, "Tell them that we are in emergency." The copilot radioed the control tower, and again did not use the word *emergency*.

"We're running out of fuel," he stated matter-of-factly. The controller replied, "I'm going to bring you in about 15 miles northeast and then turn you back onto the approach—Is that fine with you and your fuel?" Copilot Klotz said, "I guess so."

Cavides, still having trouble hearing the radio, asked anxiously, "What did he say?" The flight engineer broke in at this point with his interpretation, "The guy is angry."

Captain Cavides did not care who was angry. He needed to land the plane.

The control tower then gave turning directions to another nearby flight, a TWA plane. Confused, Captain Cavides started to make the wrong turn—the turn intended for the TWA pilot. It was a full 15 seconds before the control tower realized what was happening and got Avianca Flight 52 back on the correct heading. Those 15 seconds wasted more fuel, and Flight 52 was still another 15 seconds away from the airport.

Suddenly, one engine and then the other three on the Boeing 707 failed. Flight 52 began to fall from the sky. It was headed straight toward a wooded hillside. Terrified passengers sat frozen in total darkness, since the cabin had lost all electrical power. The plane first grazed the tops of tall trees. Then it chopped its way through tree trunks. The right wing was sheered completely off, and the jet's nose broke in two. It plowed up a lawn and finally skidded to a stop a mere 20 feet from a house.

There was no fire, no explosion. Investigators later interpreted this to mean that the plane had, in fact, been completely out of fuel when it crashed.

Residents of Glen Cove and nearby communities rushed to the disaster scene. They found Avianca's cabin strewn with dead and critically injured people. Victims were heaped one on top of the other. Of the 161 people aboard the flight, 73 were dead. In the eerie darkness, screams, moans, and pleas for help could be heard. Parents searched for their children, and children cried for their parents. Flight 52 had an unusually high number of infants on board. Many American couples had recently adopted children in Colombia and were returning home. In a few hours, some of these children had become orphans for the second time in their young lives.

No one will ever know for certain what went wrong with Flight 52. Crucial information was lost when all three crew members died on impact. Investigators did find, however, that Avianca's instruments showed there was enough fuel for 15 more minutes of flying. But those same investigators also reported that all the fuel lines were completely dry. The investigation left many questions unanswered. Did Captain Cavides believe he had enough fuel to land at Kennedy Airport? Why didn't he tell the tower himself of the fuel emergency? And why did he gamble with the fuel when he could have landed elsewhere? ■

If you have been timed while reading this selection, enter your reading time below. Then turn to the Words-per-Minute table on page 154 and look up your reading speed (words per minute). Enter your reading speed on the graph on page 156.

READING TIME: Unit 1

———— : ————

Minutes   *Seconds*

How well did you read?

- *Answer the four types of questions that follow. The directions for each type of question tell you how to mark your answers.*

- *When you have finished all four exercises, check your work by using the answer key on page 150. For each right answer, put a check mark (✓) on the line beside the box. For each wrong answer, write the correct answer on the line.*

- *For scoring each exercise, follow the directions below the questions.*

A FINDING THE MAIN IDEA

Look at the three statements below. One expresses the main idea of the story you just read. A good main idea statement answers two questions: it tells *who* or *what* is the subject of the story, and it answers the understood question *does what?* or *is what?* Another statement is *too broad;* it is vague and doesn't tell much about the topic of the story. The third statement is *too narrow;* it tells about only one part of the story.

Match the statements with the three answer choices below by writing the letter of each answer in the box in front of the statement it goes with.

M—Main Idea   B—Too Broad   N—Too Narrow

____ ☐ 1. There will always be questions about why Avianca Flight 52 ran out of fuel and crashed.

____ ☐ 2. Seventy-three people died when Avianca Flight 52 crashed into a wooded hillside.

____ ☐ 3. Air traffic controllers did not understand the trouble aboard Flight 52.

____ Score 15 points for a correct *M* answer
____ Score 5 points for each correct *B* or *N* answer

____ TOTAL SCORE: Finding the Main Idea

B RECALLING FACTS

How well do you remember the facts in the story you just read?
Put an *x* in the box in front of the correct answer to each of the
multiple-choice questions below.

1. Flight 52 experienced delays
   - ☐ a. while still in Colombia.
   - ☐ b. because of engine trouble.
   - ☐ c. while over Virginia and New Jersey.

2. The Avianca crew was concerned that
   - ☐ a. they might be carrying cocaine.
   - ☐ b. their passengers would arrive late.
   - ☐ c. they were running dangerously low on fuel.

3. Most flights into JFK Airport that night
   - ☐ a. landed in Boston instead.
   - ☐ b. turned back.
   - ☐ c. circled until the weather improved.

4. Flight 52 wasted more fuel when the pilot
   - ☐ a. stopped to search for cocaine.
   - ☐ b. followed instructions meant for another plane.
   - ☐ c. couldn't find Kennedy Airport.

5. The control tower
   - ☐ a. was fully aware of Flight 52's fuel shortage.
   - ☐ b. kept the Avianca crew on hold.
   - ☐ c. did not understand the flight was in danger.

Score 5 points for each correct answer

____ TOTAL SCORE: Recalling Facts

C MAKING INFERENCES

An inference is a judgment that is made or an idea that is arrived
at based on facts or on information that is given. You make an
inference when you understand something that is *not* stated
directly but that is *implied*, or suggested, by the facts that are given.

Below are five statements that are judgments or ideas that have
been arrived at from the facts of the story. Write the letter *C* in
the box in front of each statement that is a correct inference. Write
the letter *F* in front of each faulty inference.

C—Correct Inference   F—Faulty Inference

1. ☐ If the copilot had used the word *emergency* the crash might not have occurred.

2. ☐ Flight 52 experienced an unusual number of delays.

3. ☐ Captain Cavides and his copilot made some serious mistakes.

4. ☐ The passengers were unaware of the fuel shortage.

5. ☐ Investigators found cocaine in the cockpit.

Score 5 points for each correct answer

____ TOTAL SCORE: Making Inferences

D USING WORDS PRECISELY

Each of the numbered sentences below contains an underlined word or phrase from the story you have just read. Under the sentence are three definitions. One is a *synonym*, a word that means the same or almost the same thing: *big* and *large*. One is an *antonym*, a word that has the opposite or nearly opposite meaning: *love* and *hate*. One is an unrelated word; it has a completely *different* meaning. Match the definitions with the three answer choices by writing the letter that stands for each answer in the box in front of the definition it goes with.

S—Synonym   A—Antonym   D—Different

1. Smugglers <u>constantly</u> used the airline to carry cocaine. . . .

   ____ ☐ a. frequently

   ____ ☐ b. seldom

   ____ ☐ c. faithfully

2. In a calm and confident voice, he told the control tower that Flight 52 needed a <u>priority</u> landing because of low fuel.

   ____ ☐ a. slow and gradual

   ____ ☐ b. earlier

   ____ ☐ c. immediate and urgent

3. But the control tower did *not* understand just how <u>critical</u> Flight 52's fuel problem really was.

   ____ ☐ a. insignificant

   ____ ☐ b. serious

   ____ ☐ c. fault-finding

4. And the situation worsened when another controller took over <u>monitoring</u> the flight.

   ____ ☐ a. guarding

   ____ ☐ b. observing

   ____ ☐ c. forgetting about

5. They found Avianca's cabin <u>strewn</u> with dead and critically injured people.

   ____ ☐ a. spread

   ____ ☐ b. neatly positioned

   ____ ☐ c. scattered

____ Score 3 points for each correct *S* answer

____ Score 1 point for each correct *A* or *D* answer

____ TOTAL SCORE: Using Words Precisely

● *Enter the four total scores in the spaces below, and add them together to find your Critical Reading Score. Then record your Critical Reading Score on the graph on page 157.*

_____ Finding the Main Idea
_____ Recalling Facts
_____ Making Inferences
_____ Using Words Precisely
_____ CRITICAL READING SCORE: Unit 1

Custer's Last Stand

The hot June sun glared down on Custer and his 225 weary soldiers. Time was running out, and Custer knew their only chance to survive was to charge the hill in front of them. Behind them, Chief Gall and 1,500 warriors were already attacking.

Custer may have paused to glance up at the crest of the hill. If he did, he would have seen that Crazy Horse and at least 1,000 warriors had reached the crest before him. The Sioux and Cheyenne had the Seventh Cavalry surrounded, and now they closed in.

As the smoke from the guns and the clouds of churning dust cleared, only a few white men remained standing. Dead and dying men and horses covered the slope near the Little Bighorn River. Custer was one of the few troopers still on his feet. But in 20 minutes or less, the battle would be over. Custer and every soldier with him would be dead.

* * *

Probably no other battle in the history of the United States has caused more controversy than the Battle of the Little Bighorn. Why did Custer suffer such a crushing defeat? That's the question historians have been asking for over a century.

George Armstrong Custer always wanted to be a soldier. In 1861 he graduated last in his class from West Point. But during the Civil War he quickly proved that he was a fearless leader. By the age of 23 he was made a brigadier general. Two years later he became a major general.

Many who served with the "boy general" in the war thought he was a brave man. Yet many others felt he was too proud, overbearing, and a "glory hunter." They resented his flashy style. Instead of the army uniform, he had a fringed buckskin suit specially made. And he often disobeyed orders.

But now the Civil War was over. The army was smaller and didn't need as many generals. Custer was cut in rank to lieutenant colonel. He was assigned second-in-command of the newly formed Seventh Cavalry.

The main task of the army was to protect the crews building the railroads in the West and to deal with the Plains Indians. In 1874 Custer marched into the Black Hills for an exploratory trip. After surveying the area, Custer sent a scout back to the fort with a news release: Gold in the Black Hills! But years earlier a treaty had given that land to the Sioux. No white person could use the land without the permission of the Sioux.

The desire for gold proved too strong. In less than a year thousands of miners and their families poured into the region. The government wanted the Sioux to sell their land.

The Sioux refused to sell. They banded together with the Cheyenne near the Little Bighorn River. In their camp of thousands of men, women, and children there were at least 3,000 warriors.

Custer wanted to battle the Sioux and Cheyenne. He felt that a victory was the only way to restore his reputation with President Ulysses S. Grant. Custer had served under Grant during the war. But recently Custer had angered the president. Grant's brother had been involved in a scandal, and Custer had testified against him. An enraged Grant took away Custer's command.

At last Custer's friend, Major General Alfred Terry, persuaded Grant to let Custer return to the Seventh and Fort Abraham Lincoln in what is now North Dakota. Grant agreed, but insisted that Terry be in command. Custer and the Seventh were now part of Terry's force. Their job was to find the Sioux-Cheyenne camp.

In June 1876 Terry's forces were to meet up with those of Colonel Gibbon and General Crook. The plan was to trap the Indians in a three-pronged attack. But Crook's forces were attacked along the way and unable to join Terry. Terry gave Custer orders to lead the Seventh to the Little Bighorn valley and *wait* for Terry and the others to join him.

Custer wanted to make sure that he won

the glory of defeating the Plains Indians. He and the Seventh made a forced-march to the Little Bighorn River. The men and their horses were exhausted. For days they rode late into the night and started again before dawn. Custer arrived at the meeting place well before schedule.

Even though Terry had ordered Custer to do nothing until the others arrived, Custer had no intention of waiting. His scouts warned him that the Sioux camp they found was larger than any they'd ever seen before. Still, Custer ignored their warnings and decided to attack with his weary troops.

Then Custer made another devastating mistake. He divided his already outnumbered Seventh. He told Captain Frederick Benteen to take 125 men and sweep south of the river valley. Major Marcus Reno was given 140 men and told by Custer, "Take your battalion and try to bring them to battle, and I will support you with the whole outfit."

Why did Custer divide his troops? Did he realize what he was asking of Reno? He was sending Reno to attack the south end of what was probably the largest group of Plains Indians ever to assemble in the American West.

Custer and his 225 men galloped into the ravine toward the Indian camp. In the meantime, Reno was under attack and waiting

George Armstrong Custer had a reputation of disobeying orders. He was also called a "glory hunter"—and rightly so. At the Battle at Little Bighorn, Custer ordered his troops to attack the Sioux and Cheyenne without waiting for the rest of the Seventh Cavalry to arrive. His search for glory cost him his life and the lives of 225 men.

for Custer to join him. Reno was a capable officer, but neither he nor his tired men had any experience fighting the Indians. The warriors outnumbered the soldiers and had better arms. The soldiers carried single-shot rifles, while the warriors had the latest Winchester repeaters.

After 20 minutes of fighting, Reno ordered a retreat. Benteen met up with Reno. Neither commands could reach Custer because they were driven back by the Sioux.

Custer and his men were trapped. And they were outnumbered by more than 10 to 1. Most of the troopers' rifles jammed, which meant the soldiers had to use a knife to dig the cases from the chambers and then reload. The Indians kept up a steady stream of weapon fire. As the ranks of soldiers thinned, the Sioux and Cheyenne moved in and killed the remaining troops with knives and hatchets. The Sioux and Cheyenne attack, directed by Sitting Bull, Crazy Horse, and Gall, ended when Custer

and all 225 men were dead. The only survivor from Custer's command was a horse named Comanche. After the attack, the Seventh saw that a badly wounded Comanche was returned to the fort. He became a symbol of the Battle at Little Bighorn.

Many feel that Custer lost the now famous battle but won the war. Soon after his defeat, the Plains Indians were forced onto reservations. They also had to sell their land. ■

If you have been timed while reading this selection, enter your reading time below. Then turn to the Words-per-Minute table on page 154 and look up your reading speed (words per minute). Enter your reading speed on the graph on page 156.

READING TIME: Unit 2
_____ : _____
Minutes   *Seconds*

Lieutenant Colonel George Armstrong Custer

How well did you read?

- *Answer the four types of questions that follow. The directions for each type of question tell you how to mark your answers.*

- *When you have finished all four exercises, check your work by using the answer key on page 150. For each right answer, put a check mark (✓) on the line beside the box. For each wrong answer, write the correct answer on the line.*

- *For scoring each exercise, follow the directions below the questions.*

A FINDING THE MAIN IDEA

Look at the three statements below. One expresses the main idea of the story you just read. A good main idea statement answers two questions: it tells *who* or *what* is the subject of the story, and it answers the understood question *does what?* or *is what?* Another statement is *too broad;* it is vague and doesn't tell much about the topic of the story. The third statement is *too narrow;* it tells about only one part of the story.

Match the statements with the three answer choices below by writing the letter of each answer in the box in front of the statement it goes with.

M—Main Idea   B—Too Broad   N—Too Narrow

_____ ☐ 1. Custer and the Seventh Cavalry fought a losing battle at Little Bighorn.

_____ ☐ 2. Historians still wonder why Custer made so many fatal decisions.

_____ ☐ 3. At least 3,000 Sioux and Cheyenne warriors were camped at Little Bighorn.

_____ Score 15 points for a correct *M* answer

_____ Score 5 points for each correct *B* or *N* answer

_____ TOTAL SCORE: Finding the Main Idea

B RECALLING FACTS

How well do you remember the facts in the story you just read? Put an *x* in the box in front of the correct answer to each of the multiple-choice questions below.

1. Custer had fought in the
   - ____ ☐ a. Civil War.
   - ____ ☐ b. Mexican War.
   - ____ ☐ c. American Revolution.

2. Custer's cavalry included Captain Benteen and
   - ____ ☐ a. Colonel Gibbon.
   - ____ ☐ b. Major Marcus Reno.
   - ____ ☐ c. Major General Alfred Terry.

3. When Reno's command began to lose the fight, they
   - ____ ☐ a. went back to the fort.
   - ____ ☐ b. retreated.
   - ____ ☐ c. surrendered.

4. The Battle of the Little Bighorn occurred in
   - ____ ☐ a. September 1875.
   - ____ ☐ b. May 1861.
   - ____ ☐ c. June 1876.

5. The Seventh Cavalry was equipped with
   - ____ ☐ a. single-shot rifles.
   - ____ ☐ b. Winchester repeaters.
   - ____ ☐ c. knives.

Score 5 points for each correct answer

____ TOTAL SCORE: Recalling Facts

C MAKING INFERENCES

An inference is a judgment that is made or an idea that is arrived at based on facts or on information that is given. You make an inference when you understand something that is *not* stated directly but that is *implied,* or suggested, by the facts that are given.

Below are five statements that are judgments or ideas that have been arrived at from the facts of the story. Write the letter *C* in the box in front of each statement that is a correct inference. Write the letter *F* in front of each faulty inference.

C—Correct Inference   F—Faulty Inference

- ____ ☐ 1. Custer will not be remembered for his skilled leadership.
- ____ ☐ 2. The Seventh Cavalry used old rifles and ammunition.
- ____ ☐ 3. Major General Terry disliked Custer.
- ____ ☐ 4. The Sioux and Cheyenne cared more about the gold than their land.
- ____ ☐ 5. Custer had a history of disobeying orders.

Score 5 points for each correct answer

____ TOTAL SCORE: Making Inferences

D USING WORDS PRECISELY

Each of the numbered sentences below contains an underlined word or phrase from the story you have just read. Under the sentence are three definitions. One is a *synonym*, a word that means the same or almost the same thing: *big* and *large*. One is an *antonym*, a word that has the opposite or nearly opposite meaning: *love* and *hate*. One is an unrelated word; it has a completely *different* meaning. Match the definitions with the three answer choices by writing the letter that stands for each answer in the box in front of the definition it goes with.

S—Synonym   A—Antonym   D—Different

1. Yet many others felt he [Custer] was too proud, too <u>overbearing</u>, and a "glory hunter."

____ ☐ a. bossy

____ ☐ b. weak

____ ☐ c. important

2. They <u>resented</u> his [Custer's] flashy style.

____ ☐ a. felt sorry for

____ ☐ b. disapproved of

____ ☐ c. welcomed

3. In 1874 Custer marched into the Black Hills for an <u>exploratory</u> trip.

____ ☐ a. useless

____ ☐ b. fact-finding

____ ☐ c. experimental

4. He felt that a victory was the only way to restore his <u>reputation</u> with President Ulysses S. Grant.

____ ☐ a. good name; character

____ ☐ b. influence

____ ☐ c. hidden qualities

5. Then Custer made another <u>devastating</u> mistake.

____ ☐ a. confusing

____ ☐ b. helpful

____ ☐ c. disastrous

____ Score 3 points for each correct S answer

____ Score 1 point for each correct A or D answer

____ TOTAL SCORE: Using Words Precisely

● *Enter the four total scores in the spaces below, and add them together to find your Critical Reading Score. Then record your Critical Reading Score on the graph on page 157.*

_____	Finding the Main Idea
_____	Recalling Facts
_____	Making Inferences
_____	Using Words Precisely
_____	CRITICAL READING SCORE: Unit 2

The fire aboard the luxury liner **Morro Castle** is a shameful story of a trusted crew's neglect and betrayal. Placing their own lives before the lives of their passengers, many crew members fled the ship when they were most needed. Yet although this is a story filled with great cowardice, it also is a tale of great heroism.

Fire on the High Seas

"What is that big ship afire off the coast at Shark River?" Several ships radioed that question to Coast Guard stations along the New Jersey coast. The Coast Guard's own shore patrols and watchtowers could see a big ship on fire only eight miles out to sea. The fire looked bad, but the ship hadn't sent an SOS or fired distress rockets.

The ship on fire was the luxury liner *Morro Castle,* completing the last part of a Havana, Cuba, to New York City trip.

The fire had begun at 3:00 A.M., just after most passengers had gone to sleep. They were tired after the traditional captain's ball, held on the last night out. Two events marred the dinner. The first spoiler was the terribly rough weather. One-third of the passengers were seasick and had spent the whole day in bed. The second event that spoiled the captain's ball was the absence of Captain R. R. Wilmott, who had collapsed and had been carried to his cabin. During the ball it was announced that the captain had died of a heart attack.

The man who succeeded Captain Wilmott was the *Morro Castle's* chief mate, First Officer William Warms. Warms was on watch on the bridge early in the morning of September 8, 1934. Suddenly, an alarm signaled a fire aboard the ship. Warms, as acting captain, should have issued several orders. First, he should have closed the ship's fire doors

to prevent the fire from spreading. Second, he should have cut the ship's speed to prevent the wind from fanning the flames and spreading them. Then, he should have sent a radio signal that his ship was having some trouble and might need help. Acting Captain Warms did none of these things. In fact, he did just the opposite. He speeded up the *Morro Castle.* With the strong wind that was already blowing, a wind of 40 knots fanned the flames. Then, Warms zigzagged the ship, causing the wind to spread the flames to all parts of the ship.

Junior Radio Operator George Alagna asked the captain several times for permission to send an SOS, but each time the captain refused.

One of the junior officers, a man named Hansen, pleaded with the captain. He wanted Warms to beach the ship on the Jersey shore, only a few miles away. Warms insisted that he could make it to New York City, 40 miles away. Hansen, fed up, shouted, "You damn fool. . . . We won't last that long." Then he punched Warms, knocking him down.

Junior Radio Operator Alagna finally wrung permission from Warms to broadcast an SOS. By this time the fire was directly under the radio shack. Alagna and Chief Radio Operator George Rogers stuck to their posts, radioing for help. The heat

was so intense that they had to wrap wet towels around their heads. The metal deck beneath their feet was actually glowing red, and Alagna and Rogers had to sit with their feet propped up on the rungs of their chairs.

The radio operators got off one SOS, then *Morro Castle* lost its power and the radio went dead. That single SOS was sufficient. The Coast Guard, alerted by the smoke and flames from the *Morro Castle,* already had a vessel on the way to the ship. They reached it 10 minutes after receiving the SOS.

Meanwhile, the crew was waiting for orders. Confused, Captain Warms ordered the anchor dropped and the ship swung about on its anchor chain only six miles from the big resort city of Asbury Park, New Jersey.

Chief Engineer Eban Abbot was up on deck. He phoned his engineers to stick to their posts, and most of them did. Abbot himself never showed up in the engine room. Instead, he got into the first lifeboat and ordered it to pull away from the *Morro Castle.* In the boat with Abbot were 31 crew members and just 1 passenger. The loading of Abbot's boat was typical of those that left the liner. The first five boats to reach shore were half empty, holding a total of 92 crew members and 6 passengers.

The heat on the *Morro Castle* was now

so intense that the floating hotel became a floating crematorium. Many people escaped the heat and flames by jumping over the ship's side. Some of them were actually on fire when they hit the water. Other people jumped because they believed that their best hope lay in swimming the six miles to shore.

Some of the lifeboats plowed right through the midst of struggling swimmers and floating bodies, without stopping to pick up the swimmers. Hungry sharks added to the horror of the situation.

The Coast Guard and a small fleet of fishing boats that had set out from shore rescued many of the swimmers. Other liners that responded to the SOS launched their lifeboats and plucked additional swimmers from the water. Despite all these heroic efforts, 134 people died—most of them passengers.

Most of the victims had burned to death within sight of the boardwalk at the Asbury Park resort. The *Morro Castle*, reduced to a burned-out hulk, drifted up on the beach just behind the Asbury Park Convention Hall.

Chief Radio Operator Rogers was hailed as a hero. He was the guest of parades and dinners in his honor, and he was paid to go on a theater tour telling audiences of his heroic adventures.

Much later, a different picture emerged. Two books, *The Morro Castle Fire* and *Fire at Sea*, present evidence that Rogers had poisoned Captain Wilmott and started the fire. The *Morro Castle* fire was not the first fire that Rogers had been suspected of: he had been arrested for arson when he was only 12 years old. Years after the ship burned, Rogers became involved in several murders and went to prison. His criminal activities led many people to consider Rogers guilty of the deaths of Captain Wilmott and the other 133 victims of the *Morro Castle* fire. But Rogers's guilt has never been proven. We'll probably never know what really happened that fateful night at sea. ■

If you have been timed while reading this selection, enter your reading time below. Then turn to the Words-per-Minute table on page 154 and look up your reading speed (words per minute). Enter your reading speed on the graph on page 156.

READING TIME: Unit 3

_____ : _____
Minutes   *Seconds*

How well did you read?

- *Answer the four types of questions that follow. The directions for each type of question tell you how to mark your answers.*

- *When you have finished all four exercises, check your work by using the answer key on page 150. For each right answer, put a check mark (✔) on the line beside the box. For each wrong answer, write the correct answer on the line.*

- *For scoring each exercise, follow the directions below the questions.*

A FINDING THE MAIN IDEA

Look at the three statements below. One expresses the main idea of the story you just read. A good main idea statement answers two questions: it tells *who* or *what* is the subject of the story, and it answers the understood question *does what?* or *is what?* Another statement is *too broad;* it is vague and doesn't tell much about the topic of the story. The third statement is *too narrow;* it tells about only one part of the story.

Match the statements with the three answer choices below by writing the letter of each answer in the box in front of the statement it goes with.

M—Main Idea   **B—Too Broad**   **N—Too Narrow**

____ ☐ 1. Bad decisions in emergency situations can result in needless loss of life.

____ ☐ 2. A total of 134 people died when the *Morro Castle* burned off the New Jersey coast.

____ ☐ 3. When the *Morro Castle* caught fire, the captain should have cut the ship's speed.

____ Score 15 points for a correct *M* answer

____ Score 5 points for each correct *B* or *N* answer

____ TOTAL SCORE: Finding the Main Idea

B RECALLING FACTS

How well do you remember the facts in the story you just read? Put an *x* in the box in front of the correct answer to each of the multiple-choice questions below.

1. The *Morro Castle* was completing a trip from
   ___ ☐ a. New Jersey to Havana, Cuba.
   ___ ☐ b. Havana, Cuba, to New Jersey.
   ___ ☐ c. Havana, Cuba, to New York City.

2. Acting Captain Warms ordered an SOS sent
   ___ ☐ a. as soon as the fire broke out.
   ___ ☐ b. just before the ship lost its electrical power.
   ___ ☐ c. when the ship was just outside of New York harbor.

3. To keep the wind from spreading the fire, Warms should have
   ___ ☐ a. faced the ship into the wind.
   ___ ☐ b. speeded up the ship.
   ___ ☐ c. slowed down the ship.

4. Chief Radio Operator Rogers
   ___ ☐ a. was convicted of setting the fire.
   ___ ☐ b. had been arrested for starting a fire when he was 12 years old.
   ___ ☐ c. left the ship in one of the first lifeboats.

5. When the fire broke out, the seas were
   ___ ☐ a. rough.
   ___ ☐ b. calm.
   ___ ☐ c. gaining strength.

Score 5 points for each correct answer

___ TOTAL SCORE: Recalling Facts

C MAKING INFERENCES

An inference is a judgment that is made or an idea that is arrived at based on facts or on information that is given. You make an inference when you understand something that is *not* stated directly but that is *implied,* or suggested, by the facts that are given.

Below are five statements that are judgments or ideas that have been arrived at from the facts of the story. Write the letter *C* in the box in front of each statement that is a correct inference. Write the letter *F* in front of each faulty inference.

C—Correct Inference   F—Faulty Inference

___ ☐ 1. Acting Captain Warms was a cool-headed man.

___ ☐ 2. Some crew members cared more about themselves than the passengers.

___ ☐ 3. The Coast Guard did not think the fire was serious.

___ ☐ 4. More lives might have been saved if Captain Warms had pulled in at Asbury Park, New Jersey.

___ ☐ 5. It's likely that the captain was poisoned.

Score 5 points for each correct answer

___ TOTAL SCORE: Making Inferences

D USING WORDS PRECISELY

Each of the numbered sentences below contains an underlined word or phrase from the story you have just read. Under the sentence are three definitions. One is a *synonym*, a word that means the same or almost the same thing: *big* and *large*. One is an *antonym*, a word that has the opposite or nearly opposite meaning: *love* and *hate*. One is an unrelated word; it has a completely *different* meaning. Match the definitions with the three answer choices by writing the letter that stands for each answer in the box in front of the definition it goes with.

S—Synonym   A—Antonym   D—Different

1. Two events <u>marred</u> the dinner.

____ ☐ a. made more enjoyable

____ ☐ b. spoiled

____ ☐ c. marked

2. The man who <u>succeeded</u> Captain Wilmott was the *Morro Castle*'s chief mate, First Officer William Warms.

____ ☐ a. came after

____ ☐ b. did a better job than

____ ☐ c. came before

3. He [Hansen] wanted Warms to <u>beach</u> the ship. . . .

____ ☐ a. head out to sea

____ ☐ b. abandon

____ ☐ c. run the ship aground

4. The heat on the *Morro Castle* was now so intense that the floating hotel became a floating <u>crematorium</u>.

____ ☐ a. where bodies are buried

____ ☐ b. where bodies are burned

____ ☐ c. where bodies are frozen

5. . . . Rogers had been arrested for <u>arson</u> when he was only 12 years old.

____ ☐ a. fire worshipping

____ ☐ b. the crime of setting fires

____ ☐ c. extinguishing fires

____ Score 3 points for each correct *S* answer

____ Score 1 point for each correct *A* or *D* answer

____ TOTAL SCORE: Using Words Precisely

● *Enter the four total scores in the spaces below, and add them together to find your Critical Reading Score. Then record your Critical Reading Score on the graph on page 157.*

_____ Finding the Main Idea
_____ Recalling Facts
_____ Making Inferences
_____ Using Words Precisely

_____ CRITICAL READING SCORE: Unit 3

Back in the days of the Roman emperors, Pompeii was a busy, fashionable, seaside resort. But in A.D. 79, Pompeii's good fortune came to an abrupt end. Nearby Mount Vesuvius erupted, releasing poisonous gas that killed all living things in Pompeii. Vesuvius also spewed out tons of volcanic ash that formed an airtight cover over the city. Under this protective cover, Pompeii slept untouched for more than 1,500 years. Today the excavated ruins reveal a way of life that ended 2,000 years ago.

Pompeii: The City That Slept for 1,500 Years

In 1595 a worker digging a tunnel near Naples, Italy, stumbled on a buried town but did nothing about exploring it. More than a hundred years passed before historians identified the buried town. It was Pompeii, an ancient Roman city that had been destroyed and abandoned in A.D. 79.

No attempt was made to uncover Pompeii for another half century. Then, in 1748, a Spanish Army engineer became convinced that the city held vast treasure. He obtained permission from the king of Naples to begin excavating the buried city. The excavations turned up treasure of a kind that the engineer never dreamed of.

Pompeii had been built on the slope of Mount Vesuvius, an inactive volcano. In A.D. 79, however, Vesuvius became very active indeed. With almost no warning, there was a tremendous explosion inside the volcano.

A black cloud shaped like a pine tree formed over Vesuvius. The cloud blotted out the sun. It was as if an eclipse had come to the area. The eruption lasted seven days. Ash, stones, and pieces of hardened lava spurted out of the volcano. On the seventh day, Vesuvius sent out gases that killed all living things within the volcano's reach.

The clouds of ash caused lightning storms and rain. Gradually, volcanic ash mixed with mud and rain to form a heavy paste.

This paste covered the city to a depth of 12 to 50 feet. It formed a hermetically sealed layer, shutting off oxygen and preventing decay. Beneath the layer of hardened volcanic ash and mud, Pompeii lay in an unbelievably good state of preservation. It was as if the city had been frozen in place. In time, an outer layer of soil covered the layer of paste.

Nearly 2,000 years later, excavators uncovered paintings inside homes that were still bright, unfaded by time. Some of the food on tables and shelves was preserved. Loaves of bread were petrified in the ovens. Jugs still held drinkable wine. Figs, raisins, and chestnuts remained in recognizable condition. Olives preserved in oil were still edible.

But the most amazing preservations were the remains of many of Pompeii's citizens. The eruption of Mount Vesuvius had given off clouds of deadly gases. The carbon monoxide in the mixture of gases was odorless, but it was deadly. People who hadn't fled from the city died where they stood. Like their possessions, their bodies were covered and preserved by the volcanic ash and mud.

Hundreds of years after Vesuvius's eruption, excavators found the petrified body of a Roman soldier. The soldier was fully armed and standing erect. He

was found at a guard post in a niche in the city wall. He had remained at his post even though a rain of ash and small stones fell from the sky.

The bodies of gladiators who were slain that day are preserved in the volcanic paste. Inside excavated temples, the petrified bodies of priests can be seen. They appear as if frozen while performing their duties.

In one home, the diggers found the stonelike remains of a man standing upright. He holds a sword in his hand, and one foot rests on a heap of gold and silver. He seems to have been protecting his wealth from looters. Near him are the bodies of five other men he struck down before he himself was killed by Vesuvius's deadly gases. The volcanic ash preserved the looters and the guardian alike.

About 5,000 Pompeians managed to escape the doomed city, and many more tried unsuccessfully to escape. Many tied pillows over their heads for protection against the falling stones and lava, and fled. People who left the city early enough reached the nearby Mediterranean Sea. From its shore they were able to escape in boats. Those who waited too long, however, found that wild tides had swept away the docks and boats, leaving them stranded. Others were struck down before they reached the water.

Not all the people in boats were trying to get away from Pompeii. Pliny the Elder was a famous writer as well as commander of the Roman fleet. He was about 200 miles from Pompeii when he heard of the volcanic cloud hanging above Vesuvius. Pliny decided to investigate. He headed for Pompeii with some of his warships. As the ships approached Vesuvius, pieces of burning rock fell on the decks of the vessels. Pliny and his crew landed. They survived the falling rocks for a day, only to be killed by poisonous gas.

More than 15,000 of Pompeii's 20,000 people perished. The petrified remains of about 700 Pompeians can be seen today. Their bodies are on display in the 160,000-acre section of the city that has been excavated.

When Pompeii was a living city, it attracted thousands of visitors. Today, the restored city attracts millions of people from all over the world. They marvel at Pompeii's preserved wonders, and for a few hours, they step back 2,000 years to the days when Roman citizens walked the city's streets and lived in its houses. ■

If you have been timed while reading this selection, enter your reading time below. Then turn to the Words-per-Minute table on page 154 and look up your reading speed (words per minute). Enter your reading speed on the graph on page 156.

READING TIME: Unit 4

_____ : _____

Minutes   Seconds

A money belt is still visible around the waist of this petrified body of a Pompeii merchant.

How well did you read?

- *Answer the four types of questions that follow. The directions for each type of question tell you how to mark your answers.*

- *When you have finished all four exercises, check your work by using the answer key on page 150. For each right answer, put a check mark (✓) on the line beside the box. For each wrong answer, write the correct answer on the line.*

- *For scoring each exercise, follow the directions below the questions.*

A FINDING THE MAIN IDEA

Look at the three statements below. One expresses the main idea of the story you just read. A good main idea statement answers two questions: it tells *who* or *what* is the subject of the story, and it answers the understood question *does what?* or *is what?* Another statement is *too broad;* it is vague and doesn't tell much about the topic of the story. The third statement is *too narrow;* it tells about only one part of the story.

Match the statements with the three answer choices below by writing the letter of each answer in the box in front of the statement it goes with.

M—Main Idea   B—Too Broad   N—Too Narrow

____ ☐ 1. Volcanic explosions have caused some of the worst disasters in history.

____ ☐ 2. Mount Vesuvius erupted for seven days, spewing ash, rocks, and lava.

____ ☐ 3. A volcanic eruption destroyed the city of Pompeii but also preserved it.

____ Score 15 points for a correct *M* answer

____ Score 5 points for each correct *B* or *N* answer

____ TOTAL SCORE: Finding the Main Idea

B RECALLING FACTS

How well do you remember the facts in the story you just read? Put an *x* in the box in front of the correct answer to each of the multiple-choice questions below.

1. The first person to discover Pompeii was
   - ____ ☐ a. looking for treasure.
   - ____ ☐ b. digging a foundation.
   - ____ ☐ c. digging a tunnel.

2. When the city was uncovered, some of Pompeii's wines
   - ____ ☐ a. were better-tasting than today's.
   - ____ ☐ b. contained no alcohol.
   - ____ ☐ c. were still drinkable.

3. When Vesuvius started to erupt, Pliny the Elder was
   - ____ ☐ a. in Pompeii.
   - ____ ☐ b. in Rome.
   - ____ ☐ c. about 200 miles away.

4. Mount Vesuvius buried Pompeii in
   - ____ ☐ a. A.D. 79.
   - ____ ☐ b. A.D. 1595.
   - ____ ☐ c. A.D. 1748.

5. Pompeii was covered in a layer of hardened
   - ____ ☐ a. ash and mud.
   - ____ ☐ b. lava.
   - ____ ☐ c. volcanic stone.

Score 5 points for each correct answer

____ TOTAL SCORE: Recalling Facts

C MAKING INFERENCES

An inference is a judgment that is made or an idea that is arrived at based on facts or on information that is given. You make an inference when you understand something that is *not* stated directly but that is *implied*, or suggested, by the facts that are given.

Below are five statements that are judgments or ideas that have been arrived at from the facts of the story. Write the letter *C* in the box in front of each statement that is a correct inference. Write the letter *F* in front of each faulty inference.

C—Correct Inference   F—Faulty Inference

- ____ ☐ 1. Gladiators had been fighting just before Vesuvius erupted.
- ____ ☐ 2. Roman soldiers were loyal to their duty.
- ____ ☐ 3. Pompeii residents were not afraid of looters breaking into their homes.
- ____ ☐ 4. Pompeii attracted more people as a living city than it does today.
- ____ ☐ 5. Volcanoes are accompanied by wild tides.

Score 5 points for each correct answer

____ TOTAL SCORE: Making Inferences

D   USING WORDS PRECISELY

Each of the numbered sentences below contains an underlined word or phrase from the story you have just read. Under the sentence are three definitions. One is a *synonym*, a word that means the same or almost the same thing: *big* and *large*. One is an *antonym*, a word that has the opposite or nearly opposite meaning: *love* and *hate*. One is an unrelated word; it has a completely *different* meaning. Match the definitions with the three answer choices by writing the letter that stands for each answer in the box in front of the definition it goes with.

S—Synonym   A—Antonym   D—Different

1. He [the engineer] obtained permission . . . to begin <u>excavating</u> the buried city.

____ ☐ a. burying

____ ☐ b. digging out

____ ☐ c. shaping

2. It [volcanic ash] formed a <u>hermetically</u> sealed layer, shutting off oxygen and preventing decay.

____ ☐ a. off by itself

____ ☐ b. airtight

____ ☐ c. exposed to air

3. Loaves of bread were <u>petrified</u> in the ovens.

____ ☐ a. softened

____ ☐ b. inactive

____ ☐ c. turned into stone

4. The soldier was fully armed and standing <u>erect</u>.

____ ☐ a. straight up

____ ☐ b. slouched over

____ ☐ c. alert

5. He [the soldier] was found at a guard post in a <u>niche</u> in the city wall.

____ ☐ a. suitable place

____ ☐ b. raised surface

____ ☐ c. hollowed-out nook

____ Score 3 points for each correct S answer
____ Score 1 point for each correct A or D answer
____ TOTAL SCORE: Using Words Precisely

● *Enter the four total scores in the spaces below, and add them together to find your Critical Reading Score. Then record your Critical Reading Score on the graph on page 157.*

____ Finding the Main Idea
____ Recalling Facts
____ Making Inferences
____ Using Words Precisely

____ CRITICAL READING SCORE: Unit 4

Thick, choking smoke filled the air. House after house, factory after factory, church after church, fell victim to the flames. The city of London was burning to the ground! Frantic people watched in disbelief as the fires continued to advance. There seemed no way to stop the destruction. Many Londoners, fearing for their lives, tossed their belongings into boats and rowed down the Thames River.

London Falls to Ashes

Just before midnight on September 2, 1666, a fire broke out in one of London's many wooden houses. Some believe it started in Thomas Fraynor's oven. Fraynor, a baker for King Charles II, and his family had been sleeping on the second floor of their Pudding Lane home. They awoke to flames and smoke. Fraynor realized there was only one way out. In a panic, he and his children raced to an upstairs window. They climbed through the opening and along a gutter to the safety of their neighbor's home. A maid working for Fraynor also tried to escape the blaze through the window. But her fear of heights caused her to slip and fall to her death in the street below.

About an hour later, unusually strong, dry winds, which had been blowing through London for days, carried the raging fire across the street. Flames ignited piles of hay and straw, and then the Star Inn caught fire. The blaze quickly spread down London streets to the wooden warehouses and sheds along the Thames (TEMZ) River. By morning it had destroyed churches, homes, taverns, and factories. It also had started to sweep across the Old London Bridge.

Dazed Londoners fled their homes throughout the night and ran into the streets. They carried their belongings on their heads or backs. Some threw their goods into boats on the river. Their city

was literally burning to the ground. The heat of the fire was so intense that the city's pavements actually glowed. Sparks flew everywhere, swirled around by the wind. After the fire's first day, thick yellow smoke blocked out the sun.

For a time it looked like Old Saint Paul's Cathedral would be spared. But each day flames crept closer and closer, and soon the landmark was surrounded by fire. The church's roof lit up first. Then streams of molten lead from the roof covering flowed down the sides of the cathedral. Because of the intense heat, stones exploded from the church walls in all directions. Huge chunks of stone and molten lead rolled down city streets making passage impossible. When the cathedral roof finally tumbled down, the shock waves could be felt throughout London.

Unfortunately, many Londoners had believed that Old Saint Paul's would survive. In fact, many bet their businesses on it. London had hundreds of booksellers, and most of them had their shops right near the cathedral. Before the fire reached the cathedral, as many books as possible had been stored in an old crypt. But Old Saint Paul's was no match for the great fire. Thousands of books went up in flames. Half-burned pages floated off into the air; some landed dozens of miles from London.

Piles of books continued to burn for a full week after the fire was officially declared out.

Although the fire started in the vicinity of London's Thames River, fire fighters did not have enough water to fight the blaze. The city got its water from the Thames by a huge water wheel. The wheel lifted water from the river to street level. But the wheel, which was made of wood, was destroyed by the fire. So the people of London organized and formed bucket brigades. They filled wooden pails at the river and passed them along from person to person. But the buckets proved useless. They could not possibly provide enough water to put out the huge fire.

Saving the Tower of London became a major concern. Large quantities of gunpowder were stored in the Tower's vaults. If the fire managed to reach the gunpowder, half of London would immediately blow up. The loss of life and property would be enormous. The gunpowder needed to be saved for another reason. It could be used to blow up buildings directly in the fire's path.

The Lord Mayor of London supervised the fire fighting efforts. He became desperate as the horrible blaze marched on. He instructed fire fighters to use poles with hooks to pull down buildings in front of the inferno. By destroying the buildings, he hoped that firebreaks would be created.

These areas should have deprived the fire of fuel. Instead, the blaze simply fed on the torn-down structures. The Lord Mayor's plan had failed. The king of England then stepped in. He decided to use gunpowder stored at the Tower of London to create the firebreaks. But his plan failed as well. These firebreaks proved no more useful at stopping the fire than pulling down the buildings with hooks had been.

Shortly after the fire began, London's goldsmiths had searched for a safe place to protect their gold. They decided to move it to the Tower of London. Just as the booksellers believed that Old Saint Paul's would be immune to the fire, the goldsmiths also believed that the Tower would be safe. But as the fire neared the building, the goldsmiths realized that the intense heat would melt the gold. They formed a human chain and passed the gold hand to hand to boats waiting on the Thames. The craft carried most of the gold across the river to safety. Meanwhile, fire fighters fought

to save the Tower of London from ruin. They won.

King Charles and his brother passed among the brave fire fighters on the streets and handed them gold coins. This may have encouraged the fire fighters, but they knew that their battle against the blaze was hopeless. On the third day of the fire, King Charles and his brother joined the bucket brigades. The royal pair helped to pass along pails of water to throw against the flames. Their help did little good.

After five dreadful days, the London fire finally burned itself out. In the end 463 acres were completely destroyed. That's the area of a large, modern city. A total of 400 streets were wiped out, and 13,000 houses burned to ashes. Nearly 100 churches and several hospitals also had fallen victim to the blaze.

Great gains, however, resulted from the fire. A law was passed requiring that all new buildings be made of brick or stone. Hand pumps replaced the wooden buckets that had been so ineffective in battling the blaze.

Modern sewers were built under the streets. They replaced filthy, open ditches that used to run down the center of every road and lane. A modern volunteer fire department was also established. But above all, the Black Death, a plague that had been killing thousands of Londoners for hundreds of years, finally ended. The fire killed off the remaining rats and their fleas that spread the dreadful disease. ■

If you have been timed while reading this selection, enter your reading time below. Then turn to the Words-per-Minute table on page 154 and look up your reading speed (words per minute). Enter your reading speed on the graph on page 156.

READING TIME: Unit 5

_____ : _____

Minutes   *Seconds*

How well did you read?

- *Answer the four types of questions that follow. The directions for each type of question tell you how to mark your answers.*

- *When you have finished all four exercises, check your work by using the answer key on page 150. For each right answer, put a check mark (✓) on the line beside the box. For each wrong answer, write the correct answer on the line.*

- *For scoring each exercise, follow the directions below the questions.*

A   FINDING THE MAIN IDEA

Look at the three statements below. One expresses the main idea of the story you just read. A good main idea statement answers two questions: it tells *who* or *what* is the subject of the story, and it answers the understood question *does what?* or *is what?* Another statement is *too broad;* it is vague and doesn't tell much about the topic of the story. The third statement is *too narrow;* it tells about only one part of the story.

Match the statements with the three answer choices below by writing the letter of each answer in the box in front of the statement it goes with.

M—Main Idea   **B—Too Broad**   **N—Too Narrow**

_____ ☐ 1. The Great Fire of London destroyed 13,000 homes and 463 acres.

_____ ☐ 2. A huge fire swept through London in the late 1600s and caused tremendous damage.

_____ ☐ 3. Although the Great Fire destroyed the heart of London, a better city resulted.

_____ Score 15 points for a correct *M* answer

_____ Score 5 points for each correct *B* or *N* answer

_____ TOTAL SCORE: Finding the Main Idea

B RECALLING FACTS

How well do you remember the facts in the story you just read? Put an *x* in the box in front of the correct answer to each of the multiple-choice questions below.

1. The fire started in
   - ☐ a. the king's own bakery.
   - ☐ b. the king's brother's house.
   - ☐ c. a house belonging to the king's baker.

2. The king's brother
   - ☐ a. was killed by the fire.
   - ☐ b. started the fire.
   - ☐ c. joined the bucket brigade.

3. The fire burned itself out after
   - ☐ a. four days.
   - ☐ b. five days.
   - ☐ c. three days.

4. There wasn't enough water to fight the fire because
   - ☐ a. the water wheel was destroyed by the fire.
   - ☐ b. the buckets caught on fire.
   - ☐ c. nobody was willing to join the bucket brigade.

5. One good thing that resulted from the fire was that the
   - ☐ a. people began to love King Charles II.
   - ☐ b. plague was wiped out.
   - ☐ c. king's baker learned to be more careful with fire.

Score 5 points for each correct answer

_____ TOTAL SCORE: Recalling Facts

C MAKING INFERENCES

An inference is a judgment that is made or an idea that is arrived at based on facts or on information that is given. You make an inference when you understand something that is *not* stated directly but that is *implied*, or suggested, by the facts that are given.

Below are five statements that are judgments or ideas that have been arrived at from the facts of the story. Write the letter *C* in the box in front of each statement that is a correct inference. Write the letter *F* in front of each faulty inference.

C—Correct Inference   F—Faulty Inference

- ☐ 1. Strong, dry winds helped to spread the blaze.
- ☐ 2. Londoners were probably very grateful for the Thames River.
- ☐ 3. Old Saint Paul's Cathedral was able to survive the fire because it was built of stone.
- ☐ 4. The plague spread more rapidly after the fire.
- ☐ 5. The fire was started deliberately in order to clean up the city.

Score 5 points for each correct answer

_____ TOTAL SCORE: Making Inferences

D USING WORDS PRECISELY

Each of the numbered sentences below contains an underlined word or phrase from the story you have just read. Under the sentence are three definitions. One is a *synonym*, a word that means the same or almost the same thing: *big* and *large*. One is an *antonym*, a word that has the opposite or nearly opposite meaning: *love* and *hate*. One is an unrelated word; it has a completely *different* meaning. Match the definitions with the three answer choices by writing the letter that stands for each answer in the box in front of the definition it goes with.

S—Synonym   A—Antonym   D—Different

1. Their city was <u>literally</u> burning to the ground.

____ ☐ a. thought to be true

____ ☐ b. actually true

____ ☐ c. almost true

2. The heat of the fire was so <u>intense</u> that the city's pavements actually glowed.

____ ☐ a. extremely strong

____ ☐ b. very weak

____ ☐ c. deeply felt

3. Then streams of <u>molten</u> lead from the roof covering flowed down the sides of the cathedral.

____ ☐ a. melted

____ ☐ b. old

____ ☐ c. solid

4. . . . the booksellers believed that Old Saint Paul's would be <u>immune</u> to the fire. . . .

____ ☐ a. affected by

____ ☐ b. protected against

____ ☐ c. not affected by

5. . . . the <u>plague</u> that had been killing off thousands of Londoners for hundreds of years, finally ended.

____ ☐ a. epidemic disease

____ ☐ b. cure

____ ☐ c. bother, annoy

____ Score 3 points for each correct *S* answer
____ Score 1 point for each correct *A* or *D* answer

____ TOTAL SCORE: Using Words Precisely

● *Enter the four total scores in the spaces below, and add them together to find your Critical Reading Score. Then record your Critical Reading Score on the graph on page 157.*

_____	Finding the Main Idea
_____	Recalling Facts
_____	Making Inferences
_____	Using Words Precisely
_____	CRITICAL READING SCORE: Unit 5

In the 1930s many people believed that the future of air travel rested with the mighty zeppelin. But there was one major problem—dirigibles were kept afloat by hydrogen, a highly flammable gas. When the German zeppelin **Hindenburg** exploded in the United States, everyone's worst fear came true. What caused the deadly explosion? Was it an electric spark? Sabotage? Static electricity? The fiery disaster remains a mystery to investigators.

Hindenburg: Last of the Great Dirigibles

The *Hindenburg* was a huge, modern, and powerful airship. To the people of Germany, the dirigible was a proud symbol of the German nation itself. To Adolf Hitler, it was the showpiece of the new Germany rebuilding itself after its defeat in the first World War.

Germany had every reason to be proud of the *Hindenburg*. It was the largest airship ever built. The great silver liner was more than three blocks long. It measured 804 feet from nose to rudder, marked with huge black Nazi swastikas. Since the *Hindenburg*'s launching in 1936 it had completed 37 ocean crossings.

On this crossing in May 1937, the *Hindenburg* was carrying a crew of 61 plus 97 passengers. The passengers had each paid $400, a great deal of money in those days, for the three-day trip. Their $400 let them travel in great comfort and luxury. Dinner included such delicacies as lobster. The list of wines the *Hindenburg* carried was more than a page long. No possible item for the passengers' comfort or safety had been overlooked.

Passengers had to give up their own matches and cigarettes when they came aboard the airship. The *Hindenburg*'s great silver gasbag was filled with hydrogen, a highly flammable gas. The crew was taking no chances. To prevent accidental fire, smoking was permitted only in one completely fireproof room. Metal ladders and railings were encased in rubber to prevent sparks. These precautions resulted in an enviable safety record. No accident had occurred in 14 years of commercial dirigible flights.

This flight had started without a hitch. The *Hindenburg* was, however, several hours behind schedule after bucking strong headwinds over the Atlantic. In addition, mooring (tying the airship to a mast) was being delayed by heavy rain. Despite weather conditions, the *Hindenburg* had already passed over New York City and was approaching Lakehurst, about 60 miles from New York City. The *Hindenburg* had tied up at Lakehurst on all previous flights to the United States, and the navy was waiting for it on this trip. Dozens of marines and sailors were on hand to pull in the mooring lines let down from the zeppelin. These long ropes would hold it down until its nose could be secured to the mooring mast.

As the airship settled gracefully to the ground, the Lakehurst crew moved forward. Waiting behind them were more than a thousand spectators who had come, despite the rain, to watch the *Hindenburg* moor. The crowd included newspaper and movie photographers, reporters, and the friends and relatives of arriving passengers. They all watched the airship float down like a feather.

Boom!

There was an explosion and a flash of light from near the *Hindenburg*'s tail. In seconds, the airship had become a great, flaming torch. The huge black swastikas on its tail disappeared in flames. The fiery zeppelin slowly settled to the ground. Members of the ground crew scrambled for their lives. Burning pieces of the *Hindenburg*'s fabric covering fluttered to the ground among the navy men still below the dirigible as it continued its descent.

One passenger, Joseph Spahs, an acrobat, leaped to the ground from an open window. He landed unburned and completely unhurt. Other passengers and crew members also leaped from the flaming dirigible and lived. Some, however, were killed by the fall. Others survived the jump only to die later from burns suffered before they leaped.

Sailors and marines who had fled from the downward path of the fiery dirigible returned heroically to the airship to pull people from the wreckage. These sailors and marines are credited with saving many lives. One passenger, his clothes completely burned off, was met by the navy men as he walked away from the flames. "I'm completely all right," he said. Then he dropped dead.

The *Hindenburg*'s two captains, Ernst Lehmann and Max Pruss, were the last to jump from the flaming wreckage. The *Hindenburg* had had two captains on its fateful trip. Captain Lehmann had commanded the airship on its first voyages. Captain Pruss was in command during this last flight. The hair and clothing of both men were aflame as they left the dirigible's control car. Captain Pruss, though badly burned, lived. Captain Lehmann was not as lucky. Lehmann had been a dirigible pioneer. He had commanded the German zeppelins that had bombed London during the first World War. Now, the terribly burned Lehmann kept repeating, "I shall live. I shall live."

Despite his statement, Captain Lehmann died within 24 hours. The captain did live long enough, however, to offer his view that the explosion had been caused by sabotage—by a deliberately placed bomb.

People still speculate about the cause of the explosion. The official explanation of the Zeppelin Transport Company, which operated the airship, is that static electricity caused by the rainstorm ignited the explosive hydrogen.

One member of the United States ground crew had a different explanation. He saw a ripple—a sort of flutter—in the fabric near the *Hindenburg*'s tail. That flutter may have been caused by escaping hydrogen gas as it passed over the zeppelin's skin. Then, when the engines were thrown into reverse to assist in the landing, sparks were thrown off. Several observers saw sparks that could easily have ignited the flammable gas.

What really caused the explosion? Was it escaping hydrogen? Sabotage? Static electricity? We will probably never know the truth. One terrible truth is known; the end of the *Hindenburg* brought an end to the lives of 36 people. It also brought to an end the age of the giant dirigibles. ∎

If you have been timed while reading this selection, enter your reading time below. Then turn to the Words-per-Minute table on page 154 and look up your reading speed (words per minute). Enter your reading speed on the graph on page 156.

READING TIME: Unit 6

_____ : _____
Minutes   *Seconds*

How well did you read?

- *Answer the four types of questions that follow. The directions for each type of question tell you how to mark your answers.*

- *When you have finished all four exercises, check your work by using the answer key on page 150. For each right answer, put a check mark (✓) on the line beside the box. For each wrong answer, write the correct answer on the line.*

- *For scoring each exercise, follow the directions below the questions.*

A FINDING THE MAIN IDEA

Look at the three statements below. One expresses the main idea of the story you just read. A good main idea statement answers two questions: it tells *who* or *what* is the subject of the story, and it answers the understood question *does what?* or *is what?* Another statement is *too broad;* it is vague and doesn't tell much about the topic of the story. The third statement is *too narrow;* it tells about only one part of the story.

Match the statements with the three answer choices below by writing the letter of each answer in the box in front of the statement it goes with.

M—Main Idea   B—Too Broad   N—Too Narrow

_____ ☐ 1. The *Hindenburg* explosion ended 36 lives and the commercial use of the dirigible.

_____ ☐ 2. The pride of Germany went down in the *Hindenburg*'s flames.

_____ ☐ 3. The black swastikas on the *Hindenburg*'s rudder disappeared in the flames.

_____ Score 15 points for a correct *M* answer
_____ Score 5 points for each correct *B* or *N* answer

_____ TOTAL SCORE: Finding the Main Idea

B RECALLING FACTS

How well do you remember the facts in the story you just read?
Put an x in the box in front of the correct answer to each of the
multiple-choice questions below.

1. Smoking was limited aboard the *Hindenburg* because
   - ___ ☐ a. Hitler did not approve of smoking.
   - ___ ☐ b. hydrogen is very flammable.
   - ___ ☐ c. there were no fire extinguishers.

2. The *Hindenburg* arrived late because of
   - ___ ☐ a. safety precautions.
   - ___ ☐ b. strong headwinds.
   - ___ ☐ c. engine trouble.

3. The Zeppelin Transport Company believed the fire
   resulted from
   - ___ ☐ a. sabotage.
   - ___ ☐ b. a hydrogen leak near the tail.
   - ___ ☐ c. static electricity.

4. When the flaming dirigible began to sink to the ground,
   United States sailors and marines
   - ___ ☐ a. continued to stand beneath it.
   - ___ ☐ b. ran to safety but came back to rescue people.
   - ___ ☐ c. refused to help the *Hindenburg*'s passengers
     and crew.

5. The *Hindenburg* had completed
   - ___ ☐ a. 37 ocean crossings.
   - ___ ☐ b. 40 ocean crossings.
   - ___ ☐ c. 10 ocean crossings.

Score 5 points for each correct answer

___ TOTAL SCORE: Recalling Facts

C MAKING INFERENCES

An inference is a judgment that is made or an idea that is arrived
at based on facts or on information that is given. You make an
inference when you understand something that is *not* stated
directly but that is *implied*, or suggested, by the facts that are given.

Below are five statements that are judgments or ideas that have
been arrived at from the facts of the story. Write the letter *C* in
the box in front of each statement that is a correct inference. Write
the letter *F* in front of each faulty inference.

C—Correct Inference   F—Faulty Inference

- ___ ☐ 1. The *Hindenburg* crew did not follow safety rules.
- ___ ☐ 2. Traveling by airship was risky but popular.
- ___ ☐ 3. The *Hindenburg*'s passengers were wealthy.
- ___ ☐ 4. Captains Lehmann and Pruss were selfish people.
- ___ ☐ 5. Most of the victims who died were killed in the
  explosion itself.

Score 5 points for each correct answer

___ TOTAL SCORE: Making Inferences

D USING WORDS PRECISELY

Each of the numbered sentences below contains an underlined word or phrase from the story you have just read. Under the sentence are three definitions. One is a *synonym*, a word that means the same or almost the same thing: *big* and *large*. One is an *antonym*, a word that has the opposite or nearly opposite meaning: *love* and *hate*. One is an unrelated word; it has a completely *different* meaning. Match the definitions with the three answer choices by writing the letter that stands for each answer in the box in front of the definition it goes with.

S—Synonym   A—Antonym   D—Different

1. Dinner included such <u>delicacies</u> as lobster.

____ ☐ a. plain, ordinary food

____ ☐ b. special tasty food

____ ☐ c. appetizers

2. Metal ladders and railings were <u>encased</u> in rubber to prevent sparks.

____ ☐ a. locked up

____ ☐ b. exposed

____ ☐ c. completely covered

3. These precautions resulted in an <u>enviable</u> safety record.

____ ☐ a. jealous

____ ☐ b. desirable

____ ☐ c. unwanted

4. Lehmann had been a dirigible <u>pioneer</u>.

____ ☐ a. a person who does something first

____ ☐ b. a person who does something last

____ ☐ c. an early settler

5. People still <u>speculate</u> about the cause of the explosion.

____ ☐ a. take a business risk

____ ☐ b. wonder or think about

____ ☐ c. refuse to consider

____ Score 3 points for each correct *S* answer

____ Score 1 point for each correct *A* or *D* answer

____ TOTAL SCORE: Using Words Precisely

● *Enter the four total scores in the spaces below, and add them together to find your Critical Reading Score. Then record your Critical Reading Score on the graph on page 157.*

_____ Finding the Main Idea
_____ Recalling Facts
_____ Making Inferences
_____ Using Words Precisely

_____ CRITICAL READING SCORE: Unit 6

In 1889 the old South Fork Dam burst, sending a massive wave 125 feet high crashing toward Johnstown, Pennsylvania. The raging waters swept up everything—huge freight cars, houses, schools, and deadly debris like razor-sharp barbed wire. Over 4.5 billion gallons of water filled the unsuspecting town. Those who didn't drown died in the fire that engulfed the floating wreckage of their homes.

Take to the Hills!
The Johnstown Dam Is Going!

The rider galloped at top speed down the hill and on into the valley, through the pouring rain. "The dam is going!" A few residents of Johnstown, Pennsylvania, took the rider's advice—and lived. Thousands of people, however, either never got the rider's message or chose to disregard it. Many of those who didn't heed the warning paid with their lives.

The citizens of Johnstown in 1889 had good reason for ignoring the advice. Once a year the old South Fork Dam seemed about to burst. The cry, "Take to the hills," had become an annual false alarm.

This time, however, the rider who carried the warning should have been taken in earnest. The rider was John G. Parke, a civil engineer who was in charge of the dam.

The Great South Fork Dam was a huge earthen dike holding the waters of an artificial lake. The dam had been constructed without any stone or cement. It had been built by piling layer upon layer of soil, until the dam was 100 feet high. It was 90 feet wide at the base.

The dam had passed through the hands of a series of owners. In recent years the dam and the lake behind it had been bought by a group of millionaires. The millionaires called themselves the Great South Fork Fishing and Hunting Club. They spent thousands of dollars stocking the lake with

fish. They also added screens to prevent the fish from getting out through the dam's drainage holes.

Fishing was good, and the lake had never been higher than that spring of 1889. May had been an unusually rainy month. The streets in the lower parts of Johnstown were already flooded with six feet of water. Behind the dam, the lake had been rising at the rate of one foot per hour. The owners of the fishing club sent workers to pile more dirt on top of the dam to keep it from overflowing. The owners also ordered the workers to remove the screens, which had become jammed with fish, sticks, and other debris. The workers tried hard to clear the jam, but John Parke's trained engineer's eye could see that their efforts would be useless. Parke saddled a horse and began his Paul Revere ride through the valley.

The rain continued to pour. At noon, the water washed over the top of the dam. Almost immediately a big notch developed in the top of the dike. Then, according to witnesses, the whole dam simply disappeared. One minute there was a dam—the next minute, nothing. The lake moved into the valley like a living thing. In little more than half an hour, the dam emptied completely, sending 4.5 *billion* gallons of water down the valley toward Johnstown. A wave of water reaching 125 feet high raced toward

the city, leaping forward at the rate of 22 feet per second.

The huge wall of water approached East Conemaugh, a suburb of Johnstown. As it did, railroad engineer John Hess looked up from the string of freight cars his locomotive was pushing. He saw the water bearing down on him, now moving at 50 miles per hour. Hess moved the locomotive's throttle to wide open. Still pushing a string of freight cars before him, he raced the advancing flood into East Conemaugh. Hess tied down the locomotive's whistle, and its screaming blast preceded the train into the village. Johnstown was a railroad city. People in the whole Johnstown area knew that a tied-down whistle could only mean a disaster. And the already flooded streets told them what kind of disaster it was. Many people who had ignored earlier warnings now headed for the hills. Unable to reach the center of Johnstown, railroader Hess jumped from the locomotive cab in East Conemaugh, ran into his house, and roused his family. The Hesses made their way up the side of a hill just before the flood hit the village.

As the great tumbling hill of water roared on toward the center of Johnstown, it ran into the East Conemaugh rail yard. In the yard was a roundhouse containing 37 locomotives. The onrushing flood swept away both roundhouse and engines. The rush of waters was so forceful that it carried the locomotives, weighing 40 tons each, on top of the flood.

The rolling mountain of water, now filled with locomotives, freight cars, houses, trees, horses, and humans, rushed on. A great cloud of dust and moisture rolled before the racing floodwaters. The dust cloud was so heavy that many residents of Johnstown never saw the rolling flood-waters behind it. The cloud was quickly named the *death mist*.

The mountain of water continued its headlong rush. Just before it reached Johnstown, it destroyed the Gautier Wire Works. The buildings of the wire works and its hundreds of miles of flesh-piercing barbed wire were added to the swirling debris.

The giant rolling hill of water rushed into the heart of Johnstown. The flood swept into two distinct parts like the arms of the letter Y. One arm of the flood roared through the residential part of town. Churches, schools, and houses gave way before its power; 800 homes were flushed away.

The second arm of the flood, a tumbling mass of houses, trains, people, and animals, swept up to a stone bridge that spanned the valley. The debris caught in the bridge's stone arches and became wedged there. A collection of hundreds of parts of buildings and thousands of residents became hope-lessly bound in coils of barbed wire. The water formed a great swirling whirlpool behind them. Hundreds of additional people had approached the whirlpool on makeshift rafts made from pieces of wreckage. They leaped onto the swirling debris, joining the people already trapped there.

Then a new horror broke out. Many stoves, their fires still burning, floated into and ignited the mass of debris. Residents on the bridge overhead and on the nearby shore managed to rescue some people by reaching for them with long poles and ropes. Thousands of victims found themselves trapped between the still rising water and the flames. Some accounts of the flood claim that 200 people committed suicide by deliberately jumping into the flames. They were just a few of the 2,000 to 7,000 people believed to have lost their lives at Johnstown.

A week after the flood, a demolitions expert placed nine 50-pound cases of dynamite in the debris and cleared the jam. The waters were free to pass under the bridge and continue the 75-mile trip down the valley to Pittsburgh. The people of that city made an astonishing find. The floodwaters had carried a piece of wooden flooring from Johnstown to Pittsburgh. On that bit of wreckage, completely unhurt by the wild ride, was a healthy five-month-old baby. ■

If you have been timed while reading this selec-tion, enter your reading time below. Then turn to the Words-per-Minute table on page 154 and look up your reading speed (words per minute). Enter your reading speed on the graph on page 156.

READING TIME: Unit 7

_____ : _____
Minutes   Seconds

How well did you read?

- *Answer the four types of questions that follow. The directions for each type of question tell you how to mark your answers.*

- *When you have finished all four exercises, check your work by using the answer key on page 150. For each right answer, put a check mark (✓) on the line beside the box. For each wrong answer, write the correct answer on the line.*

- *For scoring each exercise, follow the directions below the questions.*

A FINDING THE MAIN IDEA

Look at the three statements below. One expresses the main idea of the story you just read. A good main idea statement answers two questions: it tells *who* or *what* is the subject of the story, and it answers the understood question *does what?* or *is what?* Another statement is *too broad;* it is vague and doesn't tell much about the topic of the story. The third statement is *too narrow;* it tells about only one part of the story.

Match the statements with the three answer choices below by writing the letter of each answer in the box in front of the statement it goes with.

M—Main Idea   B—Too Broad   N—Too Narrow

_____ ☐ 1. Some people tried to escape the Johnstown flood by making rafts from the wreckage.

_____ ☐ 2. Johnstown was destroyed by a flood when an earthern dam gave way.

_____ ☐ 3. The Johnstown flood resulted from a combination of human error and natural causes.

_____ Score 15 points for a correct *M* answer

_____ Score 5 points for each correct *B* or *N* answer

_____ TOTAL SCORE: Finding the Main Idea

B RECALLING FACTS

How well do you remember the facts in the story you just read? Put an *x* in the box in front of the correct answer to each of the multiple-choice questions below.

1. Some people didn't believe the dam had burst because
   - ___ ☐ a. flooding was common in Johnstown.
   - ___ ☐ b. there had been too many false alarms.
   - ___ ☐ c. it looked strong enough to last.

2. The number of victims who lost their lives in the flood was
   - ___ ☐ a. 2 to 700.
   - ___ ☐ b. 2,000 to 7,000.
   - ___ ☐ c. 200,000 to 700,000.

3. The dam was owned by the
   - ___ ☐ a. East Conemaugh Railroad.
   - ___ ☐ b. Gautier Wire Works.
   - ___ ☐ c. Great South Fork Fishing and Hunting Club.

4. Wreckage caught in a stone bridge caused the floodwaters to
   - ___ ☐ a. form a whirlpool.
   - ___ ☐ b. switch channels.
   - ___ ☐ c. catch on fire.

5. Many people didn't see the flood coming because
   - ___ ☐ a. it was hidden by a dust cloud.
   - ___ ☐ b. it moved so rapidly.
   - ___ ☐ c. they were sleeping.

Score 5 points for each correct answer

___ TOTAL SCORE: Recalling Facts

C MAKING INFERENCES

An inference is a judgment that is made or an idea that is arrived at based on facts or on information that is given. You make an inference when you understand something that is *not* stated directly but that is *implied*, or suggested, by the facts that are given.

Below are five statements that are judgments or ideas that have been arrived at from the facts of the story. Write the letter *C* in the box in front of each statement that is a correct inference. Write the letter *F* in front of each faulty inference.

C—Correct Inference   F—Faulty Inference

- ___ ☐ 1. Putting screens over the dam's drainage holes was a mistake.
- ___ ☐ 2. More lives could have been saved if the locomotive had reached Johnstown earlier.
- ___ ☐ 3. The millionaires of the Great South Fork Fishing and Hunting Club did nothing to prevent the flood.
- ___ ☐ 4. Johnstown residents didn't believe the dam would burst.
- ___ ☐ 5. Civil engineer John Parke did his best to warn the residents about the flood.

Score 5 points for each correct answer

___ TOTAL SCORE: Making Inferences

D USING WORDS PRECISELY

Each of the numbered sentences below contains an underlined word or phrase from the story you have just read. Under the sentence are three definitions. One is a *synonym*, a word that means the same or almost the same thing: *big* and *large*. One is an *antonym*, a word that has the opposite or nearly opposite meaning: *love* and *hate*. One is an unrelated word; it has a completely *different* meaning. Match the definitions with the three answer choices by writing the letter that stands for each answer in the box in front of the definition it goes with.

S—Synonym   A—Antonym   D—Different

1. Thousands of people . . . chose to <u>disregard</u> the message.

    ____ ☐ a. heed

    ____ ☐ b. forget

    ____ ☐ c. ignore

2. This time, however, the rider who carried the warning should have been taken in <u>earnest</u>.

    ____ ☐ a. seriously

    ____ ☐ b. a token

    ____ ☐ c. lightly

3. . . . John Parke's <u>trained</u> engineer's eye could see that their efforts would be useless.

    ____ ☐ a. educated

    ____ ☐ b. unskilled

    ____ ☐ c. thoughtful

4. The mountain of water continued its <u>headlong</u> rush.

    ____ ☐ a. steep

    ____ ☐ b. deliberate; reckless

    ____ ☐ c. backward

5. The debris caught in the bridge's stone arches and became <u>wedged</u> there.

    ____ ☐ a. packed in tightly

    ____ ☐ b. forced apart

    ____ ☐ c. held loosely

____ Score 3 points for each correct *S* answer

____ Score 1 point for each correct *A* or *D* answer

____ TOTAL SCORE: Using Words Precisely

● *Enter the four total scores in the spaces below, and add them together to find your Critical Reading Score. Then record your Critical Reading Score on the graph on page 157.*

_____	Finding the Main Idea
_____	Recalling Facts
_____	Making Inferences
_____	Using Words Precisely
_____	CRITICAL READING SCORE: Unit 7

GROUP TWO

"God Himself couldn't sink the Titanic," somebody once said. Yet sink it did—and before it had even completed its first trip. On that day in 1912, many refused to believe the Titanic was in trouble. Passengers kept celebrating and the band continued to play ragtime. The gallant band switched to a solemn hymn, however, when the end was near. As the unsinkable Titanic descended into its watery grave, 1,500 passengers trembled at their fate. Below (inset) is the midget sub Alvin, which discovered and photographed the Titanic in its final resting place—two and a half miles below the ocean's surface.

Death of the Unsinkable *Titanic*

"The safest ship afloat." "A seagoing hotel!" "Unsinkable!" These were the words the newspapers used in writing about the *Titanic*, the largest ship ever built.

The year was 1912. The *Titanic* was on its first trip. It was sailing that April from Southampton, England, to New York City. The captain of the British ship was E. J. Smith, a veteran of many years of transatlantic service. Smith wanted to prove that the *Titanic* was not only the world's most luxurious ship but also the fastest. Smith held the *Titanic* to 22 knots for most of the voyage.

The *Titanic* carried the very latest in wireless equipment. It received messages from two nearby ships. They warned that they had seen many icebergs. In spite of the warnings, the *Titanic* continued at 22 knots.

Lookout Fred Fleet peered ahead from his position high up on the mast. He could see a huge bulk looming in the *Titanic*'s path. Iceberg! Fleet struck three bells—the signal for something dead ahead. First Officer Murdoch, on watch on the bridge, ordered *hard-a-starboard*. Almost at the same instant, Murdoch signaled the engine room to stop. The *Titanic* turned to one side, seeming to take forever. Too late! With a long, grinding sound, the *Titanic* scraped along the side of the iceberg. The passengers felt almost no shock. The blow was a glancing one; it was almost a near miss. Pieces of ice rained down on one of the *Titanic*'s decks. The passengers, in a holiday mood, felt no sense of danger. After all, everyone knew the *Titanic* was unsinkable. Besides, the crash had been a mere scrape. Card players continued their games. Some passengers sent waiters to pick up chunks of ice from the deck. They used the ice to cool their drinks.

Down in the engine room, the crew could see that the *Titanic*'s hurt was serious. The berg had ripped a long, jagged gash below the vessel's waterline. The sea was pouring in.

The *Titanic* had compartments that divided it into sections from bow to stern. It had been designed so that if any compartment were holed, watertight doors could shut off that section. The undamaged compartments would be more than enough to keep the ship afloat. If the *Titanic* had struck the iceberg head on, damage would have been much less. At worst, the bow and the first couple of watertight compartments would have been damaged. When the *Titanic* turned to avoid the berg, however, its hull scraped along the berg. A jagged underwater spur of ice had slashed a 300-foot wound in the *Titanic*'s side. Water was pouring into too many of the watertight sections.

In 10 minutes, the water in the forward part of the ship was 8 feet deep. Though the ship's pumps had been started up, they were of little help. Below in the firerooms, half-naked, sweating stokers shoveled coal. They fed the great furnaces of the *Titanic*'s boilers. Those boilers supplied power for the pumps and provided electricity for the lights and the wireless.

The engineers and stokers were fighting a losing battle. Water was flooding in much too fast for the pumps. Slowly, the engine room crew retreated before the advancing water. Many of the boilers were flooded out. Enough, however, kept working to furnish electricity for the lights and the wireless.

The *Carpathia*, hours away, heard the *Titanic*'s SOS. The *Carpathia* doubled the number of stokers feeding the furnaces. It sent a wireless message to the *Titanic*: "Coming hard!"

Titanic's captain gave the order to abandon ship. The old rule of the sea—women and children first—was sounded. Not many passengers responded to it. People simply would not believe that the *Titanic*, with its double bottom and watertight compartments, could sink. Many women refused to be parted from their husbands. As a result, the first lifeboats pulled away from the ship only half filled.

The sinking *Titanic* was bathed in the

glow of distress rockets that it fired every few minutes. Passengers began to understand that the impossible was actually happening. The *Titanic* was going down! The lifeboats were now heavily loaded. And when people realized there would not be nearly enough room in the boats for all of them, they began to panic.

The *Titanic*'s bow was deep under water. Its stern rose in the air. The screws—those gigantic propellers that had driven the ship toward a new speed record and toward disaster—were swinging up. Finally they were completely pulled out of the water.

People in the lifeboats could see, by the glare of the *Titanic*'s lights, the hundreds of passengers left to their fate aboard the ship. The occupants of the boats watched with a grim fascination. They could see their doomed husbands, relatives, and friends aboard the now rapidly sinking ship. With a great final shudder, the *Titanic* stood on end. Then it plunged beneath the sea.

The lifeboats had moved away from the *Titanic*. They wanted to avoid being pulled down by the suction of the sinking ship. The people in the lifeboats assessed their situation. The *Titanic* had been carrying over 2,200 passengers. The lifeboats had a capacity of 1,178. However, in the confusion and in the disbelief that the ship would sink, only 711 people had secured places in the boats.

Twenty minutes after the *Titanic* had slid under the sea, the *Carpathia* arrived on the scene in response to the *Titanic*'s SOS. The *Carpathia*'s searchlight probed the night expecting to find the great ship. But the beams of light picked up only small boats—some all but empty—bobbing about on the sea. The unsinkable *Titanic* had carried over 1,500 people with it to a watery grave. The *Carpathia* took the 711 survivors aboard. Then the liner headed for New York at its best speed.

The *Titanic* and the passengers and crew members it carried lay undisturbed in their watery grave for almost three quarters of a century. Over those long years, many expeditions searched for the remains of the *Titanic*. In 1986, *Alvin*, a midget sub designed for deep-water exploration, joined the search. *Alvin* succeeded in finding the *Titanic*'s rusty remains. The liner lay in two pieces, more than two and one-half miles down. The ship's bow had plunged 50 feet into the muddy bottom before settling down into the sand. The rear half of the ship, badly broken up, lay some distance away. Scattered about the wreckage for some distance were reminders of the passengers it had carried. Video cameras aboard *Alvin* scanned the sea bottom. They picked up images of bottles of champagne, china cups and saucers, and the head of a little girl's doll.

The crew of the midget sub placed a bronze tablet near the *Titanic*'s stern. The marker is in memory of the 1,522 lost souls who perished with the great ship. May the *Titanic* and they Rest in Peace. ■

If you have been timed while reading this selection, enter your reading time below. Then turn to the Words-per-Minute table on page 155 and look up your reading speed (words per minute). Enter your reading speed on the graph on page 156.

READING TIME: Unit 8

——————— : ———————
Minutes   *Seconds*

How well did you read?

- *Answer the four types of questions that follow. The directions for each type of question tell you how to mark your answers.*

- *When you have finished all four exercises, check your work by using the answer key on page 151. For each right answer, put a check mark (✓) on the line beside the box. For each wrong answer, write the correct answer on the line.*

- *For scoring each exercise, follow the directions below the questions.*

A FINDING THE MAIN IDEA

Look at the three statements below. One expresses the main idea of the story you just read. A good main idea statement answers two questions: it tells *who* or *what* is the subject of the story, and it answers the understood question *does what?* or *is what?* Another statement is *too broad;* it is vague and doesn't tell much about the topic of the story. The third statement is *too narrow;* it tells about only one part of the story.

Match the statements with the three answer choices below by writing the letter of each answer in the box in front of the statement it goes with.

M—Main Idea   B—Too Broad   N—Too Narrow

____ ☐ 1. Icebergs can do tremendous damage to ships.

____ ☐ 2. Over 1,500 people died when the *Titanic* sank after hitting an iceberg.

____ ☐ 3. An iceberg slashed a 300-foot gash in the *Titanic*'s side.

____ Score 15 points for a correct *M* answer
____ Score 5 points for each correct *B* or *N* answer

____ TOTAL SCORE: Finding the Main Idea

B RECALLING FACTS

How well do you remember the facts in the story you just read? Put an x in the box in front of the correct answer to each of the multiple-choice questions below.

1. The *Titanic* was speeding along at 22 knots because
   - a. the captain wanted to prove it was the world's fastest ship.
   - b. the crew was unaware that there were icebergs nearby.
   - c. it was running late.

2. The *Titanic* may not have had as much damage if
   - a. it had not swerved to avoid the berg.
   - b. there had been lookouts on duty.
   - c. it had carried wireless equipment.

3. The iceberg
   - a. crushed the *Titanic*'s bow and first compartments.
   - b. crushed the *Titanic*'s stern.
   - c. slashed open many of the *Titanic*'s watertight compartments.

4. The *Titanic*'s pumps
   - a. were too small for such a large ship.
   - b. couldn't keep up with the huge amounts of water pouring in.
   - c. were out of order.

5. The first lifeboats left the ship only half full because
   - a. passengers were afraid to board them.
   - b. people didn't believe the *Titanic* was sinking.
   - c. the crew didn't want them overcrowded.

Score 5 points for each correct answer

____ TOTAL SCORE: Recalling Facts

C MAKING INFERENCES

An inference is a judgment that is made or an idea that is arrived at based on facts or on information that is given. You make an inference when you understand something that is *not* stated directly but that is *implied,* or suggested, by the facts that are given.

Below are five statements that are judgments or ideas that have been arrived at from the facts of the story. Write the letter *C* in the box in front of each statement that is a correct inference. Write the letter *F* in front of each faulty inference.

C—Correct Inference   F—Faulty Inference

1. The *Titanic* should not have been traveling so fast.

2. The engineers and stokers couldn't believe the *Titanic* was going to sink.

3. Passengers showed good judgment when they refused to leave in the first lifeboats.

4. As the *Titanic* was sinking, it created a dangerous situation.

5. The rescuing ship, *Carpathia*, expected to arrive before the *Titanic* went under.

Score 5 points for each correct answer

____ TOTAL SCORE: Making Inferences

D USING WORDS PRECISELY

Each of the numbered sentences below contains an underlined word or phrase from the story you have just read. Under the sentence are three definitions. One is a *synonym*, a word that means the same or almost the same thing: *big* and *large*. One is an *antonym*, a word that has the opposite or nearly opposite meaning: *love* and *hate*. One is an unrelated word; it has a completely *different* meaning. Match the definitions with the three answer choices by writing the letter that stands for each answer in the box in front of the definition it goes with.

S—Synonym   A—Antonym   D—Different

1. [Captain] Smith wanted to prove that the *Titanic* was not only the world's most underlined luxurious ship but also the fastest.

    ____ ☐ a. poor and dull

    ____ ☐ b. smoothest

    ____ ☐ c. rich and splendid

2. A jagged underwater spur of ice had slashed a 300-foot wound in the *Titanic*'s side.

    ____ ☐ a. sharp, pointed growth

    ____ ☐ b. wooden brace

    ____ ☐ c. small, rounded bump

3. The occupants of the boats watched with a grim fascination.

    ____ ☐ a. sympathy

    ____ ☐ b. lack of interest

    ____ ☐ c. strong attraction

4. The people in the lifeboats assessed their situation.

    ____ ☐ a. ignored

    ____ ☐ b. took stock of

    ____ ☐ c. fixed the amount of

5. However, . . . only 711 people had secured places in the boats.

    ____ ☐ a. held

    ____ ☐ b. lost

    ____ ☐ c. anchored

____ Score 3 points for each correct *S* answer
____ Score 1 point for each correct *A* or *D* answer

____ TOTAL SCORE: Using Words Precisely

● *Enter the four total scores in the spaces below, and add them together to find your Critical Reading Score. Then record your Critical Reading Score on the graph on page 157.*

_____	Finding the Main Idea
_____	Recalling Facts
_____	Making Inferences
_____	Using Words Precisely
_____	CRITICAL READING SCORE: Unit 8

Italy's **Frecce Tricolori** *flying team assembled into position. The daredevils intended to perform one of their dazzling stunts at the Ramstein, Germany, air show. Nine of the speeding jets split into two groups to form the loops of a heart. As they headed toward one another trailing red, white, and green smoke, the crowd eagerly awaited the breathtaking feat. But as the tenth jet, the flying arrow, pierced through the heart of the formation, something went terribly wrong.*

Arrows' Deadly Fall to Earth

There's nothing like an air show to attract a crowd on a warm, sunny summer afternoon. At the United States air base at Ramstein, Germany, more than 300,000 people passed through the gates on August 28, 1988. They hurried along with picnic baskets and barbecue grills, anxious to claim a good viewing spot.

Ramstein, the largest air base in western Europe, had invited crack precision flying teams to perform for the public at its annual open house. These highly trained daredevils knew what the crowd expected—lots of speed, noise, and thrilling acrobatic stunts. The exhibition promised great entertainment.

As the first flying team took off that afternoon, spectators craned their necks skyward. They watched aviators from France and Portugal perform their daring maneuvers and responded with tumultuous applause. Now it was time for the last event of the day, featuring the Italian *Frecce Tricolori* (Tricolor Arrows) team. The Arrows had been Italy's top flying team for almost 60 years. Each pilot had thousands of hours of flying experience. But despite their skill, the team had a reputation for being reckless. One member of France's precision team said the Arrows "push too far."

The Italian team flew jets that had been modified. The wingtip fuel tanks were removed so that the planes could fly even closer together—each wingtip practically brushing the next plane's wingtip.

For the Arrows' grand finale, 10 MB-339A attack jets roared down the runway. The brightly painted jets reached a speed of 350 miles per hour. About 4:00 P.M. they swept over the field on their last flyby. They were barely 100 feet above the ground. The pilots went into formation for "the arrow through the heart," a flashy stunt and supposedly an easy one. Nine of the planes split into two groups and made the loops for the heart. Then they headed straight at one another, trailing red, white, and green smoke, the colors of the Italian flag. The last jet, the "arrow," made a single loop, which would take it through the bottom of the heart.

In clear view of the crowd, the tenth jet collided with two other planes. One of the jets fell to the ground tail first, then cartwheeled into the spectators and exploded. The second plane crashed onto the runway, while the third smashed into nearby woods. All three pilots were killed. At first many spectators couldn't believe their eyes.

German television crews had been filming the exhibition live. The cameras now aired the fiery display in all its horror, including the screams of the injured. Several cars were afire, and black smoke mushroomed from the scene. Spectators—many with their hair and clothing burned from their bodies—staggered about. Dozens lay dead on the ground, their bodies blackened by kerosene burns from the flaming jet fuel. Ambulances and rescue helicopters converged on the air base. Victims were taken to civilian hospitals and to the United States Air Force hospital at Ramstein.

It was the worst air show accident in history. The final death toll was 49. Some 500 people were injured.

German officials and residents reacted with anger. For years they had been troubled by the ground-hugging maneuvers practiced by the jets stationed at the American air base. At least 20 fighter jets had crashed near the base, several in populated areas. The Germans wanted to ban the low-flying exercises, saying they were too dangerous. Residents joined local churches in requesting that the air shows be canceled. Before the 1988 air show at Ramstein, protesters stood outside the gates of the air base carrying cards that read, "We are afraid of the air shows. End them now."

Air show disasters have a long history in Germany. Five years before the Ramstein nightmare, a Canadian jet fighter crashed at another German air show. The falling jet struck a car, killing a minister and his two children. In September 1982 an American helicopter exploded at an exhibition. Forty-six people were killed.

Other countries have had tragedies at air shows as well. In England in 1952 a plane broke up, and an engine fell into the crowd, killing 28 people and injuring 63. In France, a year before the Ramstein disaster, an Airbus carrying 133 joyriders stalled, plowed into a forest, and burned. Through some miracle, only three people died. And just 25 minutes before the Arrows' crash, a Finnish pilot dived to his death at an air show in Belgium.

Despite the deadly accidents and the calls to ban air shows, exhibitions around the world continue. British, French, and Spanish officials, for example, claim their strict safety rules would prevent air show accidents. The United States Air Force and Navy claim an accident like Ramstein would not happen at their bases.

Italy announced shortly after the horrible tragedy that the Tricolor Arrows team would fly again. The nation, meanwhile, was in mourning. ∎

If you have been timed while reading this selection, enter your reading time below. Then turn to the Words-per-Minute table on page 155 and look up your reading speed (words per minute). Enter your reading speed on the graph on page 156.

READING TIME: Unit 9

——————— : ———————
Minutes   *Seconds*

How well did you read?

- *Answer the four types of questions that follow. The directions for each type of question tell you how to mark your answers.*

- *When you have finished all four exercises, check your work by using the answer key on page 151. For each right answer, put a check mark (✓) on the line beside the box. For each wrong answer, write the correct answer on the line.*

- *For scoring each exercise, follow the directions below the questions.*

check your work by using the answer key on page 151.

A   FINDING THE MAIN IDEA

Look at the three statements below. One expresses the main idea of the story you just read. A good main idea statement answers two questions: it tells *who* or *what* is the subject of the story, and it answers the understood question *does what?* or *is what?* Another statement is *too broad;* it is vague and doesn't tell much about the topic of the story. The third statement is *too narrow;* it tells about only one part of the story.

Match the statements with the three answer choices below by writing the letter of each answer in the box in front of the statement it goes with.

M—Main Idea   B—Too Broad   N—Too Narrow

_____ ☐ 1. Three pilots of Italy's *Frecce Tricolori* precision flying team were killed in an air show accident.

_____ ☐ 2. The worst air show accident in history occurred in Ramstein, Germany.

_____ ☐ 3. Three Italian pilots and many spectators were killed in an air show accident at Ramstein air base.

_____ Score 15 points for a correct *M* answer

_____ Score 5 points for each correct *B* or *N* answer

_____ TOTAL SCORE: Finding the Main Idea

B RECALLING FACTS

How well do you remember the facts in the story you just read?
Put an *x* in the box in front of the correct answer to each of the
multiple-choice questions below.

1. The *Frecce Tricolori* team was formed
   - ☐ a. especially for the air show at Ramstein.
   - ☐ b. almost 60 years before Ramstein.
   - ☐ c. more than 10 years before Ramstein.

2. German officials and residents
   - ☐ a. supported the air shows.
   - ☐ b. wanted the Ramstein base shut down.
   - ☐ c. protested against the air shows.

3. The Italian flying team
   - ☐ a. performed last.
   - ☐ b. were scheduled to perform first.
   - ☐ c. performed between the French and the
         Portuguese teams.

4. The Ramstein disaster occurred at a(n)
   - ☐ a. American air base.
   - ☐ b. German air base.
   - ☐ c. Italian air base.

5. When the collision occurred, the Arrows were
   - ☐ a. coming in for a landing.
   - ☐ b. flying in opposite directions.
   - ☐ c. completing the "arrow through the heart."

Score 5 points for each correct answer

_____ TOTAL SCORE: Recalling Facts

C MAKING INFERENCES

An inference is a judgment that is made or an idea that is arrived
at based on facts or on information that is given. You make an
inference when you understand something that is *not* stated
directly but that is *implied*, or suggested, by the facts that are given.

Below are five statements that are judgments or ideas that have
been arrived at from the facts of the story. Write the letter *C* in
the box in front of each statement that is a correct inference. Write
the letter *F* in front of each faulty inference.

C—Correct Inference   **F—Faulty Inference**

- ☐ 1. The *Frecce Tricolori* indirectly got its name from
       the colors of the Italian flag.

- ☐ 2. Bad weather contributed to the collision at
       Ramstein air base.

- ☐ 3. The Arrows' pilots were inexperienced.

- ☐ 4. Disasters at air shows rarely happen.

- ☐ 5. Some countries are confident that their air show
       safety rules can prevent accidents.

Score 5 points for each correct answer

_____ TOTAL SCORE: Making Inferences

D USING WORDS PRECISELY

Each of the numbered sentences below contains an underlined word or phrase from the story you have just read. Under the sentence are three definitions. One is a *synonym,* a word that means the same or almost the same thing: *big* and *large.* One is an *antonym,* a word that has the opposite or nearly opposite meaning: *love* and *hate.* One is an unrelated word; it has a completely *different* meaning. Match the definitions with the three answer choices by writing the letter that stands for each answer in the box in front of the definition it goes with.

S—Synonym   A—Antonym   D—Different

1. As the first flying team took off that afternoon, spectators <u>craned</u> their necks skyward.

____ ☐ a. stretched

____ ☐ b. to hesitate

____ ☐ c. relaxed

2. They watched aviators . . . perform their daring maneuvers and responded with <u>tumultuous</u> applause.

____ ☐ a. polite

____ ☐ b. noisy

____ ☐ c. tense

3. The Italian team flew jets that had been <u>modified</u>.

____ ☐ a. limited

____ ☐ b. changed a little

____ ☐ c. kept the same

4. Several cars were afire, and black smoke <u>mushroomed</u> from the scene.

____ ☐ a. moldy

____ ☐ b. fell to the ground

____ ☐ c. rose rapidly

5. Ambulances and rescue helicopters <u>converged</u> on the air base.

____ ☐ a. came together

____ ☐ b. separated

____ ☐ c. united

____ Score 3 points for each correct *S* answer

____ Score 1 point for each correct *A* or *D* answer

____ TOTAL SCORE: Using Words Precisely

● *Enter the four total scores in the spaces below, and add them together to find your Critical Reading Score. Then record your Critical Reading Score on the graph on page 157.*

____ Finding the Main Idea
____ Recalling Facts
____ Making Inferences
____ Using Words Precisely

____ CRITICAL READING SCORE: Unit 9

The Cocoanut Grove, Boston's biggest, busiest, most glamorous nightclub, was really swinging when fire unexpectedly broke out. In seconds, laughter changed to screams as flames quickly engulfed the club. People who had been dancing suddenly found themselves fleeing for their lives. Experts believe, however, that it was panic and not the fire that caused the deaths of hundreds of people.

Boston's Cocoanut Grove Ablaze

There was a tremendous crowd at Boston's Cocoanut Grove nightclub. On November 28, 1942, the club held twice its legal capacity of 500 people. The United States was involved in World War II, and the Cocoanut Grove was crowded with soldiers ready to sail for Europe, and with sailors from Boston's big naval base. Other patrons were celebrating that afternoon's football game between Holy Cross and Boston College. Warplant workers, their pockets bulging with overtime pay, rounded out the crowd.

The Cocoanut Grove, as its name suggests, was decorated to look like a South Seas paradise with bamboo and palm trees swaying under blue tropical skies. The South Seas glamour was, unfortunately, all flammable paper and cloth. The blue skies were blue satin cloth, the bamboo was made of paper, and the palm trees placed near every table and chair were also paper.

On that fateful night, one of the guests wanted the room known as the Melody Lounge to be even darker and unscrewed a light bulb from the ceiling. Stanley Tomaszewski was a 16-year-old busboy at the Cocoanut Grove. His job was to clear tables of dirty glasses and plates. When a bartender saw how dark the Melody Lounge was, he ordered the busboy to replace the missing bulb. Tomaszewski climbed up onto a chair with a bulb, but he couldn't see where to screw in the new light. He lit a match and held it up until he burned his fingers. In pain, Tomaszewski dropped the match. A paper palm tree caught fire and ignited the blue cloth sky. The fire jumped quickly from the ceiling to the paper palms and bamboo. A bartender swiped at the fire with a wet towel and then used a fire extinguisher. For a brief time the fire was confined to the Melody Lounge, the room where it started. The sparks, however, quickly spread.

Guests in the nightclub's two other lounges were unaware of any danger. Bandleader Mickey Alpert was about to open the evening's entertainment with "The Star-Spangled Banner." Suddenly, there was a cry of "Fire!" and a woman, her dress and hair ablaze, ran into the bar. In seconds, she had set a tablecloth on fire, and the flames were jumping from paper palm to paper palm. The flames spread so rapidly that people who were eating or dancing one moment, were the next moment trying to beat fire from their hair and clothing.

There was a mad rush for the doors. Some army and naval officers tried to calm the crowd, but the rush went on picking up a panicky momentum. Most of the crowd knew only one way out: the main entrance through which they had come in. It had a revolving door, and the crowd's pushing and shoving knocked the door off its axis so that it couldn't be turned either way. Later, when police and fire fighters tried to enter the club, they found the door blocked by hundreds of bodies piled high. The club had a total of a dozen doors. The other doors, however, opened inward and couldn't be opened as people pushed against them. As the doorways became blocked with bodies, people milled about, confused in the smoke and darkness.

Vocalist Bill Payne of the Alpert Band led 20 people out of the club by passing under the stage, through a refrigerator room in the basement, and out to the safety of the street.

Other people managed to escape by running upstairs to the Cocoanut Grove's roof. They then jumped onto the tops of autos parked in the streets below.

Every available vehicle was used to rush seriously wounded people to hospitals. In addition to ambulances, cars, express trucks, newspaper delivery trucks, taxis, and even a moving van were pressed into service.

The injured benefited from new methods and drugs perfected in the early days of the war. The use of blood plasma saved many lives. So, too, did the use of the new wonder drugs, sulfa and penicillin.

When Boston doctors ran out of sulfa

drugs, they put in a call to New York City. A supply of the wonder drugs was assembled and flown up to Boston, arriving there only 1 hour and 12 minutes after the call went out.

Inside the Cocoanut Grove, the fire spread so rapidly that 491 people died, mostly from smoke inhalation. In addition, over 200 other people were scarred or crippled as a result of the fire.

Boston's fire and police departments and Civil Defense workers were quick to respond to the emergency. A group of naval officers and sailors linked arms and formed a human chain to hold back the crowd of thousands that gathered. Members of the Army, Navy, and Coast Guard helped fire fighters with their hose lines. They had the fire out in one hour even though they had to force their way into the jam of bodies behind the nightclub's doors.

After the fire was out, people began to assign blame for it. The Boston newspapers blamed busboy Stanley Tomaszewski. The public disagreed. Hundreds of people wrote letters to the 16-year-old boy assuring him that the fire had not been his fault. And the Boston Fire Department, which investigated the fire, stated that it was unable to find that Tomaszewski's conduct had started the fire.

The real villain was the panic and the blind, unreasoning rush to the exits. Experts believe that if people had remained calm, there would have been few, if any, deaths. ■

If you have been timed while reading this selection, enter your reading time below. Then turn to the Words-per-Minute table on page 155 and look up your reading speed (words per minute). Enter your reading speed on the graph on page 156.

READING TIME: Unit 10

_____ : _____
Minutes   *Seconds*

How well did you read?

- *Answer the four types of questions that follow. The directions for each type of question tell you how to mark your answers.*

- *When you have finished all four exercises, check your work by using the answer key on page 151. For each right answer, put a check mark (✓) on the line beside the box. For each wrong answer, write the correct answer on the line.*

- *For scoring each exercise, follow the directions below the questions.*

A FINDING THE MAIN IDEA

Look at the three statements below. One expresses the main idea of the story you just read. A good main idea statement answers two questions: it tells *who* or *what* is the subject of the story, and it answers the understood question *does what?* or *is what?* Another statement is *too broad;* it is vague and doesn't tell much about the topic of the story. The third statement is *too narrow;* it tells about only one part of the story.

Match the statements with the three answer choices below by writing the letter of each answer in the box in front of the statement it goes with.

M—Main Idea   B—Too Broad   N—Too Narrow

_____ ☐ 1. Hundreds of people lost their lives when a nightclub caught fire.

_____ ☐ 2. Fire fighters, police officers, and members of the armed forces responded to the Cocoanut Grove fire.

_____ ☐ 3. Hundreds of people died in the panic that followed when the Cocoanut Grove caught fire.

_____ Score 15 points for a correct *M* answer

_____ Score 5 points for each correct *B* or *N* answer

_____ TOTAL SCORE: Finding the Main Idea

B   RECALLING FACTS

How well do you remember the facts in the story you just read?
Put an *x* in the box in front of the correct answer to each of the
multiple-choice questions below.

1. The Cocoanut Grove's blue skies were made of
   - ☐ a. cloth.
   - ☐ b. paper.
   - ☐ c. cellophane.

2. Busboy Stanley Tomaszewski lit a match to
   - ☐ a. trim the decorations.
   - ☐ b. see the time.
   - ☐ c. screw in a light bulb.

3. It took only an hour and 12 minutes for
   - ☐ a. fire fighters to get the blaze under control.
   - ☐ b. drugs to reach Boston from New York City.
   - ☐ c. the fire to consume the nightclub.

4. Many people were led to safety by passing under the
   stage and through the basement by
   - ☐ a. army and naval officers.
   - ☐ b. vocalist Bill Payne.
   - ☐ c. busboy Stanley Tomaszewski.

5. People had trouble fleeing the Cocoanut Grove because
   - ☐ a. the revolving door was forced off its axis.
   - ☐ b. all of the exit doors were locked.
   - ☐ c. paper palm trees blocked the exits.

Score 5 points for each correct answer

_____ TOTAL SCORE: Recalling Facts

C   MAKING INFERENCES

An inference is a judgment that is made or an idea that is arrived
at based on facts or on information that is given. You make an
inference when you understand something that is *not* stated
directly but that is *implied*, or suggested, by the facts that are given.

Below are five statements that are judgments or ideas that have
been arrived at from the facts of the story. Write the letter *C* in
the box in front of each statement that is a correct inference. Write
the letter *F* in front of each faulty inference.

C—Correct Inference   F—Faulty Inference

1. ☐ If the number of people at the Cocoanut Grove
   had been within the legal limit, the fire would
   not have occurred.

2. ☐ The owners of the nightclub were not concerned
   with fire hazards.

3. ☐ The people of Boston cared about Stanley
   Tomaszewski.

4. ☐ When a fire breaks out, it is important to stay calm.

5. ☐ Even the wonder drugs, sulfa and penicillin,
   couldn't save many fire victims.

Score 5 points for each correct answer

_____ TOTAL SCORE: Making Inferences

D USING WORDS PRECISELY

Each of the numbered sentences below contains an underlined word or phrase from the story you have just read. Under the sentence are three definitions. One is a *synonym*, a word that means the same or almost the same thing: *big* and *large*. One is an *antonym*, a word that has the opposite or nearly opposite meaning: *love* and *hate*. One is an unrelated word; it has a completely *different* meaning. Match the definitions with the three answer choices by writing the letter that stands for each answer in the box in front of the definition it goes with.

S—Synonym   A—Antonym   D—Different

1. For a brief time the fire was <u>confined</u> to the Melody Lounge. . . .

____ ☐ a. spread out

____ ☐ b. limited

____ ☐ c. jailed

2. . . . but the rush went on picking up a panicky <u>momentum.</u>

____ ☐ a. gain in speed

____ ☐ b. loss of speed

____ ☐ c. strength

3. As the doorways became blocked with bodies, people <u>milled about</u>, confused in the smoke and darkness.

____ ☐ a. moved with a purpose

____ ☐ b. moved aimlessly

____ ☐ c. socialized

4. In addition to ambulances, cars, express trucks, . . . and even a moving van were <u>pressed into service</u>.

____ ☐ a. squeezed

____ ☐ b. sent away

____ ☐ c. called to duty

5. The injured benefited from new methods and drugs <u>perfected</u> in the early days of the war.

____ ☐ a. improved significantly

____ ☐ b. without fault

____ ☐ c. made worse

____ Score 3 points for each correct *S* answer
____ Score 1 point for each correct *A* or *D* answer

____ TOTAL SCORE: Using Words Precisely

● *Enter the four total scores in the spaces below, and add them together to find your Critical Reading Score. Then record your Critical Reading Score on the graph on page 157.*

_____ Finding the Main Idea
_____ Recalling Facts
_____ Making Inferences
_____ Using Words Precisely

_____ CRITICAL READING SCORE: Unit 10

More than 100 years ago, Krakatoa, an island in the South Pacific, all but vanished in a volcanic eruption. All over the world—thousands of miles from Krakatoa—people heard the explosion. Scientists say the eruption was the loudest noise ever heard on this planet. In 1925 a small island emerged close to the remains of Krakatoa. The newcomer was appropriately named Anak Krakatoa, child of Krakatoa. In this 1960 photo, the young volcano looks threatening, but not nearly as threatening as its parent volcano did 77 years earlier.

Krakatoa: The Doomsday Crack Heard 'Round the World

In August 1883 the people of Texas heard a tremendous boom that they thought was cannon fire. What the Texans actually heard was the sound of a series of volcanic eruptions on Krakatoa, an island halfway around the world in the South Pacific. The sound from Krakatoa (now part of Indonesia) was the loudest noise in human history.

Krakatoa was a small island—only six miles square—between Java and Sumatra. It almost disappeared from the face of the earth, and the noise of its passing was heard halfway around the world. On Borneo, 350 miles from Krakatoa, the islanders believed the sound was caused by an evil spirit seeking revenge. They managed to escape from the spirit, but only by jumping off a cliff and killing themselves.

Noise was not the volcano's only way of announcing its eruption. A cloud of steam and ash rose to a height of more than 36,000 feet—more than 7 miles. A ship more than 15 miles from Krakatoa was covered with volcanic ash 15 feet deep. Ash fell on ships as far as 1,600 miles from Krakatoa and eventually covered an area of 300,000 square miles.

Some of the lava that also spewed from the volcano mixed with air and hardened into a stone called *pumice*. The air in pumice makes it so light that it floats. Pumice from Krakatoa was blown into the sea where ocean currents spread it over a large area of the Pacific. For 18 months after the eruption, ships plowed through seas covered with great chunks of floating pumice. Then the pumice stones absorbed so much water that they lost their buoyancy and sank.

The volcano's light volcanic ash and dust rose into the atmosphere where winds carried it all over the earth. Weather all over the globe was affected for months after the eruption. For an entire year, the umbrella of dust permitted only 87 percent of the usual amount of sunlight to reach the earth. For two years, the reflection of the sun on the ash in the upper atmosphere resulted in spectacular sunsets. Sunsets were blue in South America; green in Panama. The skies over the United States glowed so red that people thought the color was the result of gigantic fires. People turned in fire alarms in Poughkeepsie, New York, and in New Haven, Connecticut.

The great shock wave generated by the eruption swept completely around the world and kept right on going. It circled the globe once—twice—seven times in all.

Krakatoa's eruption was accompanied by a great earthquake. The quake jolted the seabed under the waters surrounding the island. The seas around Krakatoa rose to a temperature 60 degrees Fahrenheit above normal. A *tsunami* (soo-nah-MEE), a giant sea wave, rolled toward the island. The tsunami reached a height of 135 feet and attained a speed of 600 miles per hour.

It was this great hill of moving water that caused most of the 36,000 casualties associated with Krakatoa. The wave spread out in all directions and wiped out more than 300 villages in Southeast Asia. The tsunami picked up a gunboat and dropped it at a point 30 feet above sea level and more than a mile inland. All of the gunboat's crew members were killed.

Giant tidal waves raced from Krakatoa to all parts of the globe. Their effects were felt as far away as the English Channel, some 13,000 miles.

Krakatoa itself was torn to pieces. Five cubic miles of rock—as much as in some of the world's tallest mountains—were blown into dust. Three-fourths of the island disappeared into dust and air. Those parts of the island that didn't explode into the air sank into the sea. Parts of the island that had been a thousand feet above sea level now lay a thousand feet under the ocean.

After the eruption, the small piece of Krakatoa that was left was covered with volcanic dust. There was no grass, no

shrubs, no trees. A single red spider—
the only living thing that survived the
eruption—spun its web, a web for which
there were no more insects.

In 1925 a small peak popped up out
of the sea next to Krakatoa. More and
more of the peak emerged from the sea
until a new island was formed. The South
Pacific islanders named the newcomer
Anak Krakatoa, Child of Krakatoa. In 1928,
three years after its birth, Anak Krakatoa
had a minor eruption. The island continues
to emerge from the sea to grow larger
and larger.

What will be the fate of Anak Krakatoa?
Will it grow into a full-sized island? Will it
have a gigantic volcanic eruption? Only
time will tell. ∎

*If you have been timed while reading this selec-
tion, enter your reading time below. Then turn to
the Words-per-Minute table on page 155 and look
up your reading speed (words per minute). Enter
your reading speed on the graph on page 156.*

READING TIME: Unit 11

_____ : _____
Minutes   *Seconds*

How well did you read?

- *Answer the four types of questions that follow. The directions for each type of question tell you how to mark your answers.*

- *When you have finished all four exercises, check your work by using the answer key on page 151. For each right answer, put a check mark (✓) on the line beside the box. For each wrong answer, write the correct answer on the line.*

- *For scoring each exercise, follow the directions below the questions.*

A FINDING THE MAIN IDEA

Look at the three statements below. One expresses the main idea of the story you just read. A good main idea statement answers two questions: it tells *who* or *what* is the subject of the story, and it answers the understood question *does what?* or *is what?* Another statement is *too broad;* it is vague and doesn't tell much about the topic of the story. The third statement is *too narrow;* it tells about only one part of the story.

Match the statements with the three answer choices below by writing the letter of each answer in the box in front of the statement it goes with.

M—Main Idea   B—Too Broad   N—Too Narrow

____ ☐ 1. The effects of volcanic eruptions on Krakatoa were felt around the world.

____ ☐ 2. Krakatoa is a dramatic example of the power of volcanoes.

____ ☐ 3. Krakatoa's eruptions and the tsunami that followed resulted in 36,000 deaths.

____ Score 15 points for a correct *M* answer
____ Score 5 points for each correct *B* or *N* answer

____ TOTAL SCORE: Finding the Main Idea

B RECALLING FACTS

How well do you remember the facts in the story you just read?
Put an *x* in the box in front of the correct answer to each of the
multiple-choice questions below.

1. The tremendous eruptions on Krakatoa could be heard
   as far away as
   ___ ☐ a. Borneo.
   ___ ☐ b. Texas.
   ___ ☐ c. Java and Sumatra.

2. Volcanic ash from Krakatoa covered a ship to a depth of
   ___ ☐ a. 15 inches.
   ___ ☐ b. 15 feet.
   ___ ☐ c. 15 yards.

3. Pumice stones from Krakatoa
   ___ ☐ a. covered large portions of the Atlantic Ocean.
   ___ ☐ b. sank ships in the Pacific Ocean.
   ___ ☐ c. drifted till they became waterlogged and sank.

4. Most of the casualties were caused by
   ___ ☐ a. a giant wave.
   ___ ☐ b. volcanic ash and dust.
   ___ ☐ c. pumice stones.

5. The skies over the United States turned
   ___ ☐ a. blue.
   ___ ☐ b. red.
   ___ ☐ c. green.

Score 5 points for each correct answer

___ TOTAL SCORE: Recalling Facts

C MAKING INFERENCES

An inference is a judgment that is made or an idea that is arrived
at based on facts or on information that is given. You make an
inference when you understand something that is *not* stated
directly but that is *implied,* or suggested, by the facts that are given.

Below are five statements that are judgments or ideas that have
been arrived at from the facts of the story. Write the letter *C* in
the box in front of each statement that is a correct inference. Write
the letter *F* in front of each faulty inference.

C—Correct Inference   F—Faulty Inference

___ ☐ 1. Each time a shock wave from Krakatoa circled
         the earth it gained in strength.

___ ☐ 2. People in Poughkeepsie, New York, and
         New Haven, Connecticut, turned in fire alarms
         when they heard the explosion.

___ ☐ 3. Krakatoa sank about a thousand feet into the sea.

___ ☐ 4. The red spider that survived the explosion probably
         died soon after.

___ ☐ 5. The story suggests that it is just a matter of time
         before Krakatoa will erupt again.

Score 5 points for each correct answer

___ TOTAL SCORE: Making Inferences

D USING WORDS PRECISELY

Each of the numbered sentences below contains an underlined word or phrase from the story you have just read. Under the sentence are three definitions. One is a *synonym*, a word that means the same or almost the same thing: *big* and *large*. One is an *antonym*, a word that has the opposite or nearly opposite meaning: *love* and *hate*. One is an unrelated word; it has a completely *different* meaning. Match the definitions with the three answer choices by writing the letter that stands for each answer in the box in front of the definition it goes with.

S—Synonym   A—Antonym   D—Different

1. Some of the lava that also <u>spewed</u> from the volcano mixed with air and hardened into . . . pumice.

____ ☐ a. fell into

____ ☐ b. burst out of

____ ☐ c. soggy piece of ground

2. Then the pumice stones absorbed so much water that they lost their <u>buoyancy</u> and sank.

____ ☐ a. ability to float

____ ☐ b. heaviness

____ ☐ c. cheerfulness

3. The great shock wave <u>generated</u> by the eruption swept completely around the world. . . .

____ ☐ a. destroyed

____ ☐ b. produced electricity

____ ☐ c. caused by

4. The tsunami . . . <u>attained</u> a speed of 600 miles per hour.

____ ☐ a. lost

____ ☐ b. reached

____ ☐ c. performed

5. The island continues to <u>emerge</u> from the sea and to grow larger and larger.

____ ☐ a. flow

____ ☐ b. rise

____ ☐ c. go back

____ Score 3 points for each correct S answer
____ Score 1 point for each correct A or D answer
____ TOTAL SCORE: Using Words Precisely

● *Enter the four total scores in the spaces below, and add them together to find your Critical Reading Score. Then record your Critical Reading Score on the graph on page 157.*

_____ Finding the Main Idea
_____ Recalling Facts
_____ Making Inferences
_____ Using Words Precisely
_____ CRITICAL READING SCORE: Unit 11

It was 1917. World War I raged in Europe. Vast quantities of Allied war materials had been shipped through and stored at Halifax harbor in Nova Scotia, including deadly explosives. Halifax harbor was armed against possible German submarine and airship attacks. Yet Halifax was not prepared for a harbor accident that would ignite the tons of munitions. But that's exactly what happened. And in less than one minute, about 1,600 people were dead and over 3,000 acres destroyed.

Halifax: City Blown to Pieces

The United States and Canada shipped vast quantities of war material to the Allies during World War I. Millions of tons of munitions passed through the Canadian port of Halifax, Nova Scotia. Because the citizens of the city feared an attack by German *zeppelins* (dirigibles or airships), artillery batteries had been set along the shore. To prevent underwater attacks, antisubmarine nets had been strung at the entrance to the harbor. That harbor was reached by way of a long channel only a mile wide. The channel was appropriately named "the narrows."

On the morning of December 6, 1917, a French ship, the *Mont Blanc,* was threading its way through the channel. It was bound for Europe with a load of munitions. The *Mont Blanc* was a floating bomb. Its cargo consisted of 7,000 tons of TNT and other explosives, plus 9,000 gallons of benzene, a highly flammable liquid.

Heading toward the *Mont Blanc* in "the narrows" was a freighter, the *Imo,* returning empty from Belgium. The *Imo* blew its whistle to signal that it would pass the *Mont Blanc* to starboard. For some reason never explained, the *Imo* continued on straight toward the *Mont Blanc.* The captain of the *Mont Blanc* realized that he couldn't get his ship out of the *Imo*'s path. He did, however, manage to maneuver the vessel so that the approaching ship would not strike its cargo of TNT. The *Imo*'s bow sliced the *Mont Blanc* all the way down to the waterline. It also sliced open the *Mont Blanc*'s cargo of benzene. The highly flammable liquid spilled into the ship's hold, where it caught fire. The blazing fuel flowed toward the 7,000 tons of explosives.

The *Mont Blanc*'s crew knew that their lives depended on putting out the flames. Although the French sailors fought desperately, the rapidly spreading flames drove them back, foot by foot. The captain realized that the struggle was hopeless and gave the order to abandon ship. The crew needed no urging. They knew that it was a life or death matter to get clear of the ship before it blew up. They rowed for their lives. When their boat reached the shore, they jumped out and kept right on fleeing.

The *Mont Blanc* and its explosive cargo drifted toward the piers of Halifax. A British warship, the *High Flyer,* had been waiting to convoy the *Mont Blanc* to Europe and protect it from attack by German subs. Now the crew aboard the *High Flyer* realized that it was the city of Halifax that needed protecting— and from the *Mont Blanc.* A boatload of British sailors set out for the blazing vessel, intending to sink it before it could explode.

They reached the burning ship and had just climbed to its deck when the *Mont Blanc* blew up with a boom heard six miles away. It simply disappeared. Many citizens of Halifax were sure that the long-expected zeppelin bombing was under way. Other residents believed that the German navy had crossed the Atlantic and was shelling them.

At least two-thirds of the sailors on the ships in Halifax harbor died instantly. The *Mont Blanc*'s blast set off other explosions among the stacks of munitions on the piers. About 3,000 acres—including homes, factories, and schools—were destroyed by the explosions and the fires that followed them. Only 10 pupils out of 500 survived the blast. It is thought that a total of 1,600 people lost their lives and 8,000 were badly injured. The exact death toll will never be known, however, since some entire families were wiped out.

A telegrapher named Vincent Coleman played one of the most heroic roles that day in a city of heroes. Coleman saw a ship on fire and realized that it was the munitions ship scheduled to dock that morning. He telegraphed: "A munitions ship is on fire and headed for Pier Eight. Goodbye." It was truly goodbye for Coleman; he died in the explosion. His message, however, started help on the way within 15 minutes of the blast. People from all over Canada and from the northeastern United States sent food, blankets, cots, medical supplies, lumber, and window glass. The survivors soon had most of the things they needed.

One survivor of the disaster was the steamship, the *Imo,* which had rammed the *Mont Blanc.* When the *Mont Blanc* exploded, the *Imo* was blown clear out of the water onto the shore. The ship was rebuilt and refloated under a new name. Four years after the Halifax explosion, the *Imo* struck a reef in the South Atlantic and sank.

The city of Halifax itself emerged much better from the disaster. There was little of the rioting and looting so common in other calamities. Druggists gave away free medical supplies and restaurants provided free meals. Halifax was soon named "The City of Comrades." Working together as comrades, the survivors of Halifax soon rebuilt their town. Today's Halifax is a strong and modern city. ■

If you have been timed while reading this selection, enter your reading time below. Then turn to the Words-per-Minute table on page 155 and look up your reading speed (words per minute). Enter your reading speed on the graph on page 156.

READING TIME: Unit 12

_____ : _____
Minutes   *Seconds*

How well did you read?

- *Answer the four types of questions that follow. The directions for each type of question tell you how to mark your answers.*

- *When you have finished all four exercises, check your work by using the answer key on page 151. For each right answer, put a check mark (✓) on the line beside the box. For each wrong answer, write the correct answer on the line.*

- *For scoring each exercise, follow the directions below the questions.*

A   FINDING THE MAIN IDEA

Look at the three statements below. One expresses the main idea of the story you just read. A good main idea statement answers two questions: it tells *who* or *what* is the subject of the story, and it answers the understood question *does what?* or *is what?* Another statement is *too broad;* it is vague and doesn't tell much about the topic of the story. The third statement is *too narrow;* it tells about only one part of the story.

Match the statements with the three answer choices below by writing the letter of each answer in the box in front of the statement it goes with.

M—Main Idea   B—Too Broad   N—Too Narrow

____ ☐ 1. Transporting explosives can be very dangerous.

____ ☐ 2. A munitions ship blew up during World War I and severely damaged Halifax.

____ ☐ 3. The explosions and fires destroyed homes, factories, and schools in Halifax.

____ Score 15 points for a correct *M* answer

____ Score 5 points for each correct *B* or *N* answer

____ TOTAL SCORE: Finding the Main Idea

B RECALLING FACTS

How well do you remember the facts in the story you just read? Put an *x* in the box in front of the correct answer to each of the multiple-choice questions below.

1. The people of Halifax feared
   - ☐ a. a zeppelin raid.
   - ☐ b. an explosion in the harbor.
   - ☐ c. an invasion by the German army.

2. The *Mont Blanc*'s crew
   - ☐ a. carelessly caused the explosion.
   - ☐ b. got away safely.
   - ☐ c. were able to keep the fire under control.

3. The crew of the British warship *High Flyer* intended to
   - ☐ a. sink the *Mont Blanc* before the fire reached the TNT.
   - ☐ b. tow the *Mont Blanc* out of the harbor.
   - ☐ c. fight the fire aboard the *Mont Blanc*.

4. Telegrapher Vincent Coleman
   - ☐ a. managed to escape the blast.
   - ☐ b. started help on the way.
   - ☐ c. warned *Mont Blanc*'s crew that the ship was going to explode.

5. The *Imo* survived the explosion because the ship
   - ☐ a. sailed away before the explosion.
   - ☐ b. had no cargo and floated high in the water.
   - ☐ c. was blown onto the shore.

Score 5 points for each correct answer

____ TOTAL SCORE: Recalling Facts

C MAKING INFERENCES

An inference is a judgment that is made or an idea that is arrived at based on facts or on information that is given. You make an inference when you understand something that is *not* stated directly but that is *implied*, or suggested, by the facts that are given.

Below are five statements that are judgments or ideas that have been arrived at from the facts of the story. Write the letter *C* in the box in front of each statement that is a correct inference. Write the letter *F* in front of each faulty inference.

C—Correct Inference   F—Faulty Inference

- ☐ 1. Telegrapher Vincent Coleman knew that he was doomed.
- ☐ 2. *Mont Blanc*'s captain was a cool-headed man.
- ☐ 3. The people of Halifax were selfish and did not care about the future of their town.
- ☐ 4. Schools were located not far from the harbor.
- ☐ 5. The *Imo* was a lucky ship.

Score 5 points for each correct answer

____ TOTAL SCORE: Making Inferences

D USING WORDS PRECISELY

Each of the numbered sentences below contains an underlined word or phrase from the story you have just read. Under the sentence are three definitions. One is a *synonym*, a word that means the same or almost the same thing: *big* and *large*. One is an *antonym*, a word that has the opposite or nearly opposite meaning: *love* and *hate*. One is an unrelated word; it has a completely *different* meaning. Match the definitions with the three answer choices by writing the letter that stands for each answer in the box in front of the definition it goes with.

S—Synonym   A—Antonym   D—Different

1. A French ship, the *Mont Blanc*, was threading its way through the channel.

____ ☐ a. carefully moving

____ ☐ b. standing still

____ ☐ c. weaving together

2. He [the captain] did, however, manage to maneuver the vessel so that the approaching ship would not strike its cargo. . . .

____ ☐ a. maintain a straight course

____ ☐ b. skillfully guide

____ ☐ c. manage

3. The *High Flyer* had been waiting to convoy the *Mont Blanc* to Europe. . . .

____ ☐ a. escort or guard

____ ☐ b. abandon or desert

____ ☐ c. carry

4. The exact death toll will never be known, however, since some entire families were wiped out.

____ ☐ a. ringing of a mourning bell

____ ☐ b. number of people who escaped

____ ☐ c. number of people lost

5. Working together as comrades, the survivors of Halifax soon rebuilt their town.

____ ☐ a. friends

____ ☐ b. communists

____ ☐ c. enemies

____ Score 3 points for each correct *S* answer
____ Score 1 point for each correct *A* or *D* answer

____ TOTAL SCORE: Using Words Precisely

● *Enter the four total scores in the spaces below, and add them together to find your Critical Reading Score. Then record your Critical Reading Score on the graph on page 157.*

_____ Finding the Main Idea
_____ Recalling Facts
_____ Making Inferences
_____ Using Words Precisely

_____ CRITICAL READING SCORE: Unit 12

Everything was calm and quiet as the HMS **Birkenhead** *steamed its way alongside the coast of Africa. The British troopship was filled with soldiers, sailors, and their families. While many of them slept that night, the ship neared* **Danger Point.** *Suddenly, it ran aground on the jagged rocks! The situation proved hopeless. For 438 British soldiers and sailors, the HMS* **Birkenhead** *became their final post.*

The Heroes of HMS *Birkenhead*

*So they stood an' was still to the Birkenhead
drill, soldier and sailor too!*
　　　　　　　　　　Rudyard Kipling

The heroic deeds of the brave men aboard
the HMS *Birkenhead* so inspired English
writer Rudyard Kipling that he wrote a
poem called "The Birken'ead Drill." It tells
an amazing story of sacrifice.

* * *

In the middle of the 19th century, a
British troopship, HMS *Birkenhead,* set sail
to South Africa. On board were 480 soldiers
from 10 different regiments. The *Birkenhead*
also carried a crew of 130, a small detach-
ment of marines, the wives and children of
some of the soldiers, and a few horses.

The ship was in a big hurry—the soldiers
were desperately needed to reinforce British
troops already at war with African tribesmen. The *Birkenhead* sailed at full speed
from the British Isles. It had a steam engine
that drove its paddle wheel, and it also
carried a full set of masts and sails.

On the night of February 23, 1852, the
Birkenhead was racing down the Atlantic
coast of Africa toward its destination, the
Cape of Good Hope. The cape is located
at the continent's southern tip. The sea
that night was not very rough, and there
was little thought of risk, even as the ship
neared a place called *Danger Point.* Those
crew members who were not on duty and

all the troops were sleeping peacefully
in their bunks.

Around 2:00 A.M. disaster struck. The
Birkenhead ran aground on the rocks! Water
rushed into the forward hold, instantly
drowning many troops as they slept. In
moments everyone else rushed on deck.
They knew from the jolt that something
terrible had happened. Some soldiers had
hastily pulled on their uniforms. Others
had on their trousers and undershirts.
To avoid panic, the officers gave orders
that the troops were to be silent and obe-
dient. The men obeyed as if they were home
on their regiment's parade ground. Some
of the troops were put to work helping the
sailors clear away the wreckage that resulted
from the crash. Others were ordered to help
pump water that kept flooding in. A few
soldiers were commanded to lighten the
ship by forcing the horses over the side.
The troops loved their horses, but they
followed their orders. Those men who were
not at work at these tasks assembled into
ranks and stood *at parade.* Although many
of the men had not been in the army long,
they carried out the commands and stood
fast in their positions.

Birkenhead's captain ordered the engines
into reverse. The engines had power enough
to back the ship off the rocks. But now the
trouble really began. The jagged rocks not

only punched the hole in the ship's side
but also plugged that opening. When
this "stopper" was removed, water came
rushing in. Everyone realized that soon
the *Birkenhead* would go down.

The lifeboats were lowered into the
ocean. But the sea, which had been calm
enough for a big troopship, was too much
for the tiny boats. A falling spar, which had
broken loose from a mast, smashed one
boat. The sea swamped two more boats as
soon as they hit the water. The crew was
able to launch successfully only one big
boat and two smaller ones. Frantic women
and children filled the big boat.

The battered *Birkenhead* broke in half
and began to sink. The commander of the
ship ordered the soldiers to jump overboard
and swim for the boats. Their colonel, however, realized there were just too many troops
for the tiny boats. Even if they only hung on
to the sides of the craft they would swamp
them. He told the soldiers to continue to
stand at parade—and they did so.

The drums continued to play. Army drummers, in those days, were supposed to be at
least 16 years old. But many 14-year-olds
managed to join the army by lying about
their age. Now the drummers stood proudly
with the older soldiers and maintained their
beat. Grizzled sergeants, veterans of many
years of service, set the example for the

B RECALLING FACTS

How well do you remember the facts in the story you just read?
Put an *x* in the box in front of the correct answer to each of the
multiple-choice questions below.

1. HMS *Birkenhead* was driven by a
   - ___ ☐ a. steam engine and sails.
   - ___ ☐ b. full set of sails.
   - ___ ☐ c. steam engine.

2. The *Birkenhead* was headed for
   - ___ ☐ a. Cape Hatteras.
   - ___ ☐ b. Cape Horn.
   - ___ ☐ c. the Cape of Good Hope.

3. Water flooded the ship even faster
   - ___ ☐ a. after it backed off the jagged rocks.
   - ___ ☐ b. when the storm became more powerful.
   - ___ ☐ c. when the pumps stopped working.

4. The horses were forced over the side to
   - ___ ☐ a. keep them from running wild on the ship.
   - ___ ☐ b. lighten the ship.
   - ___ ☐ c. save them.

5. The women and children
   - ___ ☐ a. were picked up by a passing ship.
   - ___ ☐ b. managed to row to shore.
   - ___ ☐ c. drowned when their boat was swamped.

Score 5 points for each correct answer

___ TOTAL SCORE: Recalling Facts

C MAKING INFERENCES

An inference is a judgment that is made or an idea that is arrived
at based on facts or on information that is given. You make an
inference when you understand something that is *not* stated
directly but that is *implied,* or suggested, by the facts that are given.

Below are five statements that are judgments or ideas that have
been arrived at from the facts of the story. Write the letter *C* in
the box in front of each statement that is a correct inference. Write
the letter *F* in front of each faulty inference.

C—Correct Inference   F—Faulty Inference

- ___ ☐ 1. The captain should have backed the *Birkenhead* off the rocks.

- ___ ☐ 2. Rough seas made launching and boarding the lifeboats difficult and dangerous.

- ___ ☐ 3. The British army is proud of the soldiers who died aboard the *Birkenhead.*

- ___ ☐ 4. The sergeants set a poor example for the troops.

- ___ ☐ 5. Sailing at high speed through *Danger Point* did not put the *Birkenhead* at risk.

Score 5 points for each correct answer

___ TOTAL SCORE: Making Inferences

D USING WORDS PRECISELY

Each of the numbered sentences below contains an underlined word or phrase from the story you have just read. Under the sentence are three definitions. One is a *synonym,* a word that means the same or almost the same thing: *big* and *large.* One is an *antonym,* a word that has the opposite or nearly opposite meaning: *love* and *hate.* One is an unrelated word; it has a completely *different* meaning. Match the definitions with the three answer choices by writing the letter that stands for each answer in the box in front of the definition it goes with.

S—Synonym   A—Antonym   D—Different

1. . . . the soldiers were desperately needed to <u>reinforce</u> British troops already at war with African tribesmen.

   ____ ☐ a. strengthen

   ____ ☐ b. weaken

   ____ ☐ c. join

2. Those men who were not at work at these tasks assembled into ranks and stood *at parade.*

   ____ ☐ a. march around

   ____ ☐ b. stand formally at attention

   ____ ☐ c. show pride

3. Although many of the men had not been in the army long, they carried out the commands and stood <u>fast</u> in their positions.

   ____ ☐ a. swiftly

   ____ ☐ b. loosely

   ____ ☐ c. firmly

4. The sea <u>swamped</u> two more boats as soon as they hit the water.

   ____ ☐ a. submerged

   ____ ☐ b. overworked

   ____ ☐ c. raised

5. *Birkenhead*'s <u>list</u> increased. It was hard for the soldiers and officers to stay on their feet.

   ____ ☐ a. flatness

   ____ ☐ b. catalog

   ____ ☐ c. tilt

____ Score 3 points for each correct *S* answer

____ Score 1 point for each correct *A* or *D* answer

____ TOTAL SCORE: Using Words Precisely

● *Enter the four total scores in the spaces below, and add them together to find your Critical Reading Score. Then record your Critical Reading Score on the graph on page 157.*

_____ Finding the Main Idea

_____ Recalling Facts

_____ Making Inferences

_____ Using Words Precisely

_____ CRITICAL READING SCORE: Unit 13

The sight of the Hagenbeck-Wallace Circus Train pulling into a local station had long been a source of delight to children and adults alike. But a series of unfortunate coincidences in Ivanhoe, Indiana, turned this happy sight into a vision of death and destruction.

The Circus Troupe's Last Performance

During World War I, the Hagenbeck-Wallace Circus was one of the world's largest tent shows. On the night of June 22, 1918, the show was traveling from Michigan City, Indiana, to Hammond, Indiana. The circus moved with 14 flatcars carrying tents and equipment, seven animal cars, and four sleepers for the show folk. The sleepers were old-fashioned Pullman cars, built of wood and lit by gas lamps. In the sleeping cars, which were hitched to the very end of the train, were 300 circus people: clowns, acrobats, animal trainers, jugglers, and dancers. There was Nellie Jewel, the famous animal trainer; Hercules Navarro, the strongman; and Joe Coyle, the famous clown. Coyle's family had been complaining that they missed him when he traveled with the circus. So, as a special treat, Coyle's wife and children had joined him for a while. The children were overjoyed by the double thrill of seeing their father and getting to travel on the circus train.

As the train sped through the night, the crew became aware of an overheated brake box and decided to fix it. The train was passing through the town of Ivanhoe, Indiana, which had a railroad yard. The circus train pulled off the main track and onto a short track used for switching. The train was so long, however, that the last four cars—the Pullman sleeper cars holding the performers—extended back onto the main track.

The flagman of the circus train, Ernest Trimm, wasn't the least bit worried about the four Pullmans extending out onto the main track. Trimm set emergency flares back down the tracks and checked to be sure that the automatic signal lights shone red. Even without these precautions, however, there should have been no problem. No train was due to come down the track for more than an hour—more than enough time for the circus train's crew to repair the brake box and get the train on its way.

What Trimm had no way of knowing was that a special train was even then approaching. World War I was responsible for troop trains moving everywhere, carrying soldiers to training camps and to ships leaving for Europe. Alonzo K. Sargent, the engineer of the troop train, was exhausted. He had been shuttling troop trains between New York and Chicago for three days. Sargent also had been suffering from a kidney ailment and had been taking pills that contained a mild painkiller.

On that June evening in 1918, engineer Sargent's troop train had pulled out of the station early and was rolling down the track toward Ivanhoe, Indiana. Sargent was sound asleep at the throttle. He passed through three yellow caution signals without even slowing down. Sargent's fire tender, beside him in the locomotive's cab, was bent low over the firebox, feeding the boiler. He, too, failed to see the caution signals.

Flagman Trimm of the circus train, was back down the track behind his train. Trimm couldn't believe his eyes as he saw the troop train bearing down toward the circus train. He watched in disbelief as the approaching locomotive ran the three caution lights. Then, Trimm's disbelief turned to horror as the troop train, without slackening its pace, passed through a red stop signal—and kept right on going. Trimm waved his red lantern frantically. Then in a last, desperate effort, he heaved it through the engineer's window of the speeding locomotive. The thrown lantern had no effect on the sleeping engineer.

The locomotive plowed in rapid succession through the wooden sides of the first, second, third, and fourth sleeper cars of the circus train. The wooden Pullmans shattered, and the old-fashioned gas lights started fires in the wreckage.

More than 85 people died, most of them as the result of burns. Fifty-three badly burned bodies, only three of them identifiable, were buried in a single mass grave. Strongman Hercules Navarro was alive but paralyzed as a result of the crash. Clown Joe Coyle lived through the accident, but his wife and children died.

Panic broke out among the people of the nearby town of Ivanhoe, where the people believed that wild animals had escaped from their circus cages. Rumors claimed that lions and tigers were running wild through the streets. The truth, however, was that most of the animals had been in the forward section of the train, which had not been affected by the wreck. A few animals had been killed in the crash, and police later had to destroy a few other animals that had been painfully injured.

Some time after the accident, engineer Sargent was brought to trial. One of the most damaging points against the engineer was the tale told by his fire tender. Right after the crash, the fire tender had run up and down the wreckage shouting, "The engineer was asleep! The engineer was asleep!" Engineer Sargent was, nevertheless, judged to be not guilty.

On the evening after the wreck, the circus opened on schedule. Circus performers and acts from all over the country rushed to Indiana and substituted for dead and injured performers.

Truckloads of flowers from show people all over the country arrived at the circus grounds. An entire vanload of blooms arrived from the great entertainer George M. Cohan. But the flower that was best remembered was a single rose. It came from a child who had seen the show just before the crash. The card that came with the flower read: "From a little girl who laughed at your show and now cries for you." ■

If you have been timed while reading this selection, enter your reading time below. Then turn to the Words-per-Minute table on page 155 and look up your reading speed (words per minute). Enter your reading speed on the graph on page 156.

READING TIME: Unit 14

_____ : _____

Minutes   *Seconds*

How well did you read?

- *Answer the four types of questions that follow. The directions for each type of question tell you how to mark your answers.*

- *When you have finished all four exercises, check your work by using the answer key on page 151. For each right answer, put a check mark (✓) on the line beside the box. For each wrong answer, write the correct answer on the line.*

- *For scoring each exercise, follow the directions below the questions.*

A FINDING THE MAIN IDEA

Look at the three statements below. One expresses the main idea of the story you just read. A good main idea statement answers two questions: it tells *who* or *what* is the subject of the story, and it answers the understood question *does what?* or *is what?* Another statement is *too broad;* it is vague and doesn't tell much about the topic of the story. The third statement is *too narrow;* it tells about only one part of the story.

Match the statements with the three answer choices below by writing the letter of each answer in the box in front of the statement it goes with.

M—Main Idea   B—Too Broad   N—Too Narrow

_____ ☐ 1. Circus performers all over the country responded to the tragedy in Indiana.

_____ ☐ 2. Clown Joe Coyle survived the train wreck that wiped out his family.

_____ ☐ 3. A sleeping engineer ran his locomotive into a circus train, killing dozens of performers.

_____ Score 15 points for a correct *M* answer

_____ Score 5 points for each correct *B* or *N* answer

_____ TOTAL SCORE: Finding the Main Idea

B RECALLING FACTS

How well do you remember the facts in the story you just read? Put an *x* in the box in front of the correct answer to each of the multiple-choice questions below.

1. The circus train wreck occurred during
   - ☐ a. the Civil War.
   - ☐ b. World War I.
   - ☐ c. World War II.

2. The circus train stopped to
   - ☐ a. put on a special performance.
   - ☐ b. repair a brake box.
   - ☐ c. let a special troop train pass by.

3. As the oncoming locomotive passed flagman Ernest Trimm, he
   - ☐ a. set out emergency flares.
   - ☐ b. checked that the automatic signal lights were set red.
   - ☐ c. heaved his lantern through the engineer's window.

4. Entertainer George M. Cohan
   - ☐ a. rushed to Indiana and substituted for injured performers.
   - ☐ b. sent an entire vanload of blooms.
   - ☐ c. sent a single rose.

5. Clown Joe Coyle's family was traveling with him because his children
   - ☐ a. were part of his circus act.
   - ☐ b. wanted to learn to be clowns like their famous father.
   - ☐ c. missed him when he was on the circus tour.

Score 5 points for each correct answer

_____ TOTAL SCORE: Recalling Facts

C MAKING INFERENCES

An inference is a judgment that is made or an idea that is arrived at based on facts or on information that is given. You make an inference when you understand something that is *not* stated directly but that is *implied,* or suggested, by the facts that are given.

Below are five statements that are judgments or ideas that have been arrived at from the facts of the story. Write the letter *C* in the box in front of each statement that is a correct inference. Write the letter *F* in front of each faulty inference.

C—Correct Inference   F—Faulty Inference

1. ☐ The flagman for the circus train was careless.

2. ☐ Engineer Alonzo Sargent should not have worked three days in a row.

3. ☐ World War I was, in part, responsible for the train wreck.

4. ☐ Fewer people would have died or been injured if the old Pullman cars had been made of steel.

5. ☐ The placement of the sleeper cars on the main track contributed to the number of dead and injured.

Score 5 points for each correct answer

_____ TOTAL SCORE: Making Inferences

D USING WORDS PRECISELY

Each of the numbered sentences below contains an underlined word or phrase from the story you have just read. Under the sentence are three definitions. One is a *synonym,* a word that means the same or almost the same thing: *big* and *large.* One is an *antonym,* a word that has the opposite or nearly opposite meaning: *love* and *hate.* One is an unrelated word; it has a completely *different* meaning. Match the definitions with the three answer choices by writing the letter that stands for each answer in the box in front of the definition it goes with.

S—Synonym   A—Antonym   D—Different

1. In the sleeping cars, which were <u>hitched</u> to the very end of the train, were 300 circus people.

____ ☐ a. fastened

____ ☐ b. cut loose from

____ ☐ c. married

2. Even without these <u>precautions</u>, however, there should have been no problem.

____ ☐ a. safeguards

____ ☐ b. insurance

____ ☐ c. risks

3. He [the engineer] had been <u>shuttling</u> troop trains between New York and Chicago for three days.

____ ☐ a. directing

____ ☐ b. going back and forth

____ ☐ c. staying in one place

4. . . . the troop train, without <u>slackening</u> its pace, passed through a red stop signal.

____ ☐ a. speeding up

____ ☐ b. slowing up

____ ☐ c. relaxing

5. The locomotive plowed in rapid <u>succession</u> through the wooden sides of the . . . sleeper cars of the circus train.

____ ☐ a. all at once

____ ☐ b. one after the other

____ ☐ c. the order of people in line to be king or queen

____ Score 3 points for each correct *S* answer

____ Score 1 point for each correct *A* or *D* answer

____ TOTAL SCORE: Using Words Precisely

● *Enter the four total scores in the spaces below, and add them together to find your Critical Reading Score. Then record your Critical Reading Score on the graph on page 157.*

_____ Finding the Main Idea
_____ Recalling Facts
_____ Making Inferences
_____ Using Words Precisely
_____ CRITICAL READING SCORE: Unit 14

103

GROUP THREE

"Bring out your dead," wailed the town crier as huge numbers of bodies were heaped onto already packed burial carts. For more than 200 years, the Black Death spread mercilessly across Europe, sometimes wiping out entire villages. Neither religion nor medicine seemed capable of halting the disease's deadly advance. Many feared that it was indeed the end of the world.

Black Death: The End of the World

"Bring out your dead! Bring out your dead!" the driver cried as the horse-drawn carts rumbled through the streets of Europe in the 1300s. Bodies were dragged from almost every house and thrown onto the carts. Corpse was tossed on top of corpse until they were like logs in a pile of firewood. Sometimes several bodies were carried out of the same house. The Black Death had struck! One person in every three would die of the plague before it ran its course.

The Black Death was the worst calamity of all times, wiping out the entire populations of some villages. In the large city of Smolensk, Russia, only five people survived the plague. Nine out of every ten citizens of London fell victim to the Black Death. Virtually the entire populations of Iceland and Cyprus were wiped out.

So many people were struck down by the plague that the supply of coffins was soon exhausted, and the dead were carried on wooden planks to huge mass-burial pits. Corpses were piled several high, and then a thin layer of dirt was shoveled over them. Often the burials took place with no member of the family or clergy present. As people fled before the spreading plague, spouse abandoned spouse, and parents forsook children.

The plague spread quickly from person to person. People went to bed well and were dead by morning. A doctor might arrive at a home to treat a victim only to catch the plague and die before the original sufferer.

The Black Death derived its name from the color of the victim's skin in death; a person who was infected always died within three days, skin covered by black patches. There were other symptoms too. Patients developed egg-sized swellings in the groin and armpits. Sometimes victims coughed and sweated violently.

The first people to know the horror of the Black Death were the Chinese, who were hit by the plague earlier in the 14th century. The disease quickly spread to the Tartars, a people originally from the area where the present-day borders of China and the Commonwealth of Independent States (formerly the Soviet Union) meet. The Tartars, under their great leader Kipchak Janiberg, had fought their way westward across Russia. They had conquered all the Russian lands as far into Europe as the Black Sea—but they carried the plague with them.

The Tartar advance had been halted by a trading colony of Italians located in a city on the Black Sea. As more and more of Kipchak's Tartars became victims of the Black Death, he began to realize that the Italian city would never fall to him. Kipchak's troops had brought huge *catapults*, devices like giant slingshots, with them. The Tartars used them for throwing huge stones against the stone walls of forts. Kipchak had the catapults loaded with the bodies of Tartars who had died of the Black Death. The corpses were thrown over the walls and into the city, where they quickly spread the plague to the Italian colonists.

Both Italians and Tartars abandoned the city. Some of the Italians boarded a galley and rowed to Italy as fast as they could. When the galley arrived at the Italian port of Messina, the inhabitants of the port found some of the rowers dead and the remainder dying of the plague. The Black Death had come to Italy.

The plague quickly spread throughout Italy and passed on to France. From France, the plague was carried across the English Channel to Great Britain. The cycle of dead was completed when the plague spread from Britain to all the rest of Europe, sparing no country. Human survival was threatened. No wonder people said,—and believed— "This is the end of the world."

Many people believed that the plague was caused by the wrath of God. Societies of *flagellants* formed. The societies derived their name from the whips members used to beat themselves and one another. Dressed in sackcloth and ashes, the flagellants moved from town to town, beating themselves with leather whips tipped with metal points.

The flagellation made as much sense as some of the other cures proposed for the plague. The crude science of the 14th century gave no idea of either the cause of the Black Death or its cure. Thinkers came up with an idea that combined astrology, geology, and superstition. Jupiter and Mars had passed very close to Earth, and the proximity of the two planets was believed to have caused cracks in the earth's crust. The cracks, they believed, permitted poisonous fumes from the earth's center to escape and cause the plague.

Since the scientists of the time had no idea of the plague's cause, their "cures" were nearly as horrible as the disease itself. People ate and drank concoctions of blood, goat urine, lizards, toads, and boils that had been dried and powdered. Plague victims were advised to rip open the bodies of puppies and pigeons and hold the torn flesh against their plague boils. While people were vainly trying these cures, the Black Death continued its deadly passage across Europe.

The real cause of the plague had been partially discovered by an Arab physician 400 years before. The physician had noted that the plague broke out only after rats had come out of their holes to die in the open air. This observation was accurate but failed to take into account one final piece needed for the puzzle's solution—fleas. The plague germs lived and multiplied in the bodies of fleas. Every rat had hundreds of fleas that lived on rats' blood and infected them with the Black Death. When the rats died of the plague, the fleas jumped onto the nearest people. It was the bite of the fleas that spread the plague germs to their human victims.

There were house rats in every 14th-century city, so nobody was spared. The Black Death carried off king and commoner alike. It raged back and forth over Europe, on and off, for 200 years. Then gradually, it died away. (Some people think that the real end of the plague didn't come until the London Fire of 1666. That fire destroyed most of London, along with the rats, fleas, and germs that caused the plague.)

Surprisingly, during all the 200 years that the plague ravaged Europe, the cure had been at hand. The germs of the Black Death can be destroyed by the application of soap and water. ■

If you have been timed while reading this selection, enter your reading time below. Then turn to the Words-per-Minute table on page 155 and look up your reading speed (words per minute). Enter your reading speed on the graph on page 156.

READING TIME: Unit 15

_____ : _____
Minutes   *Seconds*

How well did you read?

- *Answer the four types of questions that follow. The directions for each type of question tell you how to mark your answers.*

- *When you have finished all four exercises, check your work by using the answer key on page 152. For each right answer, put a check mark (✓) on the line beside the box. For each wrong answer, write the correct answer on the line.*

- *For scoring each exercise, follow the directions below the questions.*

A FINDING THE MAIN IDEA

Look at the three statements below. One expresses the main idea of the story you just read. A good main idea statement answers two questions: it tells *who* or *what* is the subject of the story, and it answers the understood question *does what?* or *is what?* Another statement is *too broad;* it is vague and doesn't tell much about the topic of the story. The third statement is *too narrow;* it tells about only one part of the story.

Match the statements with the three answer choices below by writing the letter of each answer in the box in front of the statement it goes with.

M—Main Idea   B—Too Broad   N—Too Narrow

_____ ☐ 1. A deadly plague raced across Europe in the 14th century.

_____ ☐ 2. The Black Death, which killed millions of people in the 14th century, was spread by fleas.

_____ ☐ 3. Some people believed that the Black Death was caused by poisonous fumes escaping from the center of the earth.

_____ Score 15 points for a correct *M* answer

_____ Score 5 points for each correct *B* or *N* answer

_____ TOTAL SCORE: Finding the Main Idea

B RECALLING FACTS

How well do you remember the facts in the story you just read? Put an *x* in the box in front of the correct answer to each of the multiple-choice questions below.

1. The Black Death raged back and forth in Europe for
   - ____ ☐ a. 400 years.
   - ____ ☐ b. 200 years.
   - ____ ☐ c. 100 years.

2. Long before the plague struck Europe, an Arab physician had noted that
   - ____ ☐ a. there was a relationship between the plague and rats.
   - ____ ☐ b. soap and water were effective against the plague.
   - ____ ☐ c. there was no known cure for the disease.

3. The Tartar leader, Kipchak Janiberg, spread the plague by
   - ____ ☐ a. bringing rats and fleas to Italy.
   - ____ ☐ b. catapulting the bodies of his own men into an Italian trading colony.
   - ____ ☐ c. infecting the waters of the Black Sea.

4. The Black Death got its name from the
   - ____ ☐ a. Black Sea, where the Europeans first caught it.
   - ____ ☐ b. color of the victim's skin.
   - ____ ☐ c. Chinese, who first learned the horror of the plague.

5. The flagellants believed the plague was caused by the
   - ____ ☐ a. wrath of God.
   - ____ ☐ b. close passage of Jupiter and Mars.
   - ____ ☐ c. pigeons and puppies.

Score 5 points for each correct answer

____ TOTAL SCORE: Recalling Facts

C MAKING INFERENCES

An inference is a judgment that is made or an idea that is arrived at based on facts or on information that is given. You make an inference when you understand something that is *not* stated directly but that is *implied,* or suggested, by the facts that are given.

Below are five statements that are judgments or ideas that have been arrived at from the facts of the story. Write the letter *C* in the box in front of each statement that is a correct inference. Write the letter *F* in front of each faulty inference.

C—Correct Inference   F—Faulty Inference

- ____ ☐ 1. The plague was particularly bad in Smolensk, Russia.
- ____ ☐ 2. Although doctors couldn't cure plague victims, they did know how to protect themselves from the disease.
- ____ ☐ 3. The plague takes a long time to kill its victims.
- ____ ☐ 4. People infected by the disease were willing to try anything to survive.
- ____ ☐ 5. European cities did not control the rat population.

Score 5 points for each correct answer

____ TOTAL SCORE: Making Inferences

Each of the numbered sentences below contains an underlined word or phrase from the story you have just read. Under the sentence are three definitions. One is a *synonym*, a word that means the same or almost the same thing: *big* and *large*. One is an *antonym*, a word that has the opposite or nearly opposite meaning: *love* and *hate*. One is an unrelated word; it has a completely *different* meaning. Match the definitions with the three answer choices by writing the letter that stands for each answer in the box in front of the definition it goes with.

S—Synonym   A—Antonym   D—Different

1. One person in every three would die of the plague before it <u>ran its course</u>.

____ ☐ a. started to occur

____ ☐ b. followed a path

____ ☐ c. came to an end

2. As people fled before the spreading plague, . . . parents <u>forsook</u> children.

____ ☐ a. abandoned

____ ☐ b. rejected

____ ☐ c. came back for

3. The Black Death <u>derived</u> its name from the color of the victim's skin in death. . . .

____ ☐ a. received

____ ☐ b. inherited

____ ☐ c. gave up

4. People ate and drank <u>concoctions</u> of blood, goat urine, lizards. . . .

____ ☐ a. inventions

____ ☐ b. mixture of different ingredients

____ ☐ c. mixture of similar ingredients

5. The physician had <u>noted</u> that the plague broke out only after rats had come out of their holes to die. . . .

____ ☐ a. noticed

____ ☐ b. ignored

____ ☐ c. carefully recorded

____ Score 3 points for each correct *S* answer

____ Score 1 point for each correct *A* or *D* answer

____ TOTAL SCORE: Using Words Precisely

- *Enter the four total scores in the spaces below, and add them together to find your Critical Reading Score. Then record your Critical Reading Score on the graph on page 157.*

_____ Finding the Main Idea
_____ Recalling Facts
_____ Making Inferences
_____ Using Words Precisely

_____ CRITICAL READING SCORE: Unit 15

The Great Chicago Fire

There is an old song about how Mrs. O'Leary's cow started the Chicago Fire, and it is probably true. The O'Leary family, however, has always claimed that the fire was started by a group of boys who were smoking in the barn. One thing is certain: the biggest and worst human-made disaster in North American history started in the O'Leary barn.

In 1871 Patrick and Catherine O'Leary lived on Chicago's West Side. Patrick made a poor living carrying heavy loads by hand. Catherine added to their income with a dairy business of her own. She kept five cows in the barn behind their house and sold their milk to other families in the neighborhood.

Late in the evening of October 8, 1871, fire broke out in the O'Leary barn. According to the story told by Daniel Sullivan, the O'Learys' peg-legged neighbor, the villain was the cow who kicked over the kerosene lantern.

The hero of the story Sullivan told is—Daniel Sullivan. He rushed into the barn to try to save the cows. He managed to—although he almost fell victim to the fire himself. When Sullivan had led some of the cows to safety, the tip of his peg leg became stuck in a crack in the barn's wooden floor. As the flames closed in, Sullivan managed to pull loose barely in time to save the remaining cows—and his own life.

The Chicago Fire turned out to be such a catastrophe not only because of Mrs. O'Leary's cow but also because of the way Chicago itself was built and managed. The city had 651 miles of wooden sidewalks. There were 60,000 buildings—most of them constructed of wood. In the midst of all this wood, the fire department had 17 horse-drawn steam pumpers and 18 hook-and-ladder trucks. Although Chicago had a population of 350,000, the fire department had a force of only 200.

The night the Great Fire broke out, Chicago's fire fighters were dead tired. They had faced 30 fires during the week before, and the last fire had been an especially bad one. The fire fighters had drunk a lot of whiskey after that blaze, and many of them had hangovers. Later, some critics were to claim that many fire fighters were still drunk when the big fire broke out.

The fire department's central head-quarters was located in the city's stone "fireproof" courthouse. A fire lookout atop the courthouse's tall tower spotted smoke from the fire at the O'Leary barn and sent in the alarm. Unfortunately, the lookout reported the wrong location. By the time the correct location was discovered, the fire had gotten a solid start. The fire spread out of control, forcing citizens to flee their homes and driving everyone, including the fire department, before it. The fire fighters fought back bravely, but they had little to fight with.

The wooden buildings and sidewalks gave off millions of flying sparks, some of them the size of baseballs. And the winds resulting from the fires drove those fireballs as far as well-hit baseballs. The fireballs crossed streets and jumped over buildings and across the river, spreading the blaze.

The fire raged on. Racing before it were the looters, drunk with liquor from the saloons and stores they'd broken into. Merchants and homeowners who tried to protect their possessions were struck down—even killed. The fire moved toward Chicago's "fireproof" courthouse. Although the building was faced with a layer of limestone and its interior was marble, the heat of the fire was too intense, even for stone, and the courthouse started to go. The basement of the building housed the city's jail, where dozens of prisoners were locked up and screaming to be released. A police captain ordered the police to take the murderers outside and keep them under guard there. All other prisoners were freed.

The convicts ran down the street, unable to believe their good fortune. Their fortune really improved when they reached a well-known jewelry store. The store was already smoldering. The store's owner held out his hands to the convicts. In them he held rings, necklaces, and bracelets. "Help yourselves, gentlemen," he called. The jeweler realized that if the convicts didn't get the goods, the fire would. It made little difference to him whether the jewelry was stolen by convicts or melted by the fire. The jeweler, A. H. Miller, picked out a few of his most valuable gems and walked away with them.

People trapped in the second and third floors of houses with bottom floors on fire threw their most precious possessions to others gathered in the street. One woman dropped a large bundle of bedsheets to a man waiting below her windows. The woman quickly followed her belongings through the window, when she saw the man run off with the bundle. The bundle contained the woman's baby. The screaming mother pursued the thief as he cut in and out among the crowd, fleeing across a bridge leading from the burning city. Thief and bundle disappeared in the mass of people. The heartsick mother was thinking of leaping to her death over the railing of the bridge when she spotted her baby. He was alive, lying on some bales of cotton 10 feet below. The mother climbed down the bridge's steelwork and retrieved her infant.

The rest of Chicago did not get off so

Chicago had been a thriving commercial center when the Great Fire broke out in 1871. Made almost entirely of wood, the city quickly fell victim to the blazing demon. As citizens fled the advancing inferno, fire fighters did what little they could. But by the time the last spark was extinguished, Chicago looked like an ancient ruin, and at least 300 people were dead.

luckily. Its doom was sealed by a single burning plank carried aloft by the powerful, hot winds stirred up by the blaze. The burning plank sailed through the air until it reached the waterworks, where it crashed through the wooden roof. The waterworks had been considered fireproof, but its wooden ceiling was soon on fire. The ceiling fell onto the pumps that supplied the city with water and put them out of action. The fire fighters, left without water, were forced to give up the battle.

The fire burned out of control for 30 hours, until the early morning of October 10, 1871. Then the wind died down, and it started to rain. The rain was soon spattering onto the cinders

and charred wreckage of what had been the city of Chicago. The fire destroyed $200 million worth of buildings and left 100,000 people homeless.

Chicagoans turned their wrath on Patrick O'Leary. O'Leary, fearing for his life, escaped by dressing as a woman. He hid at a friend's house until the mob's anger died.

Chicago made a fast recovery from the fire. Six months after the blaze, half of the city had been rebuilt. In just a few years there was no sign of the fire, and the population had doubled. Hundreds of the city's new citizens were happy to buy a dramatic souvenir of the Great Fire. Many of Chicago's old-timers had discovered

that they could make money selling the hoof of the cow that kicked over the lantern and started the fire. They sold hundreds of that hoof. ■

If you have been timed while reading this selection, enter your reading time below. Then turn to the Words-per-Minute table on page 155 and look up your reading speed (words per minute). Enter your reading speed on the graph on page 156.

READING TIME: Unit 16
_____ : _____
Minutes   *Seconds*

How well did you read?

- *Answer the four types of questions that follow. The directions for each type of question tell you how to mark your answers.*

- *When you have finished all four exercises, check your work by using the answer key on page 152. For each right answer, put a check mark (✓) on the line beside the box. For each wrong answer, write the correct answer on the line.*

- *For scoring each exercise, follow the directions below the questions.*

A FINDING THE MAIN IDEA

Look at the three statements below. One expresses the main idea of the story you just read. A good main idea statement answers two questions: it tells *who* or *what* is the subject of the story, and it answers the understood question *does what?* or *is what?* Another statement is *too broad;* it is vague and doesn't tell much about the topic of the story. The third statement is *too narrow;* it tells about only one part of the story.

Match the statements with the three answer choices below by writing the letter of each answer in the box in front of the statement it goes with.

M—Main Idea   B—Too Broad   N—Too Narrow

____ ☐ 1. Thousands of people were left homeless when fire destroyed 19th-century Chicago.

____ ☐ 2. A big fire started in the O'Leary barn on Chicago's West Side when a cow kicked over a lantern.

____ ☐ 3. Chicago was the scene of the greatest human-made disaster in North America.

____ Score 15 points for a correct *M* answer
____ Score 5 points for each correct *B* or *N* answer
____ TOTAL SCORE: Finding the Main Idea

B RECALLING FACTS

How well do you remember the facts in the story you just read? Put an *x* in the box in front of the correct answer to each of the multiple-choice questions below.

1. When Daniel Sullivan entered the barn to save Mrs. O'Leary's cows
   - ___ ☐ a. the burning roof fell in on him.
   - ___ ☐ b. his peg leg got stuck in a crack in the floor.
   - ___ ☐ c. the animals refused to leave the burning building.

2. A fire spotter, whose job was to report fires,
   - ___ ☐ a. was asleep at his post.
   - ___ ☐ b. panicked and couldn't send the alarm.
   - ___ ☐ c. reported the wrong location of the fire.

3. Some sparks from the fire were as large as
   - ___ ☐ a. basketballs.
   - ___ ☐ b. golf balls.
   - ___ ☐ c. baseballs.

4. Prisoners, except for murderers, were
   - ___ ☐ a. sent to another jail.
   - ___ ☐ b. freed.
   - ___ ☐ c. put to work fighting the fire.

5. The fire was finally put out
   - ___ ☐ a. with the help of fire departments from other cities.
   - ___ ☐ b. when it started to rain.
   - ___ ☐ c. when all the wood in the city had burned.

Score 5 points for each correct answer

___ TOTAL SCORE: Recalling Facts

C MAKING INFERENCES

An inference is a judgment that is made or an idea that is arrived at based on facts or on information that is given. You make an inference when you understand something that is *not* stated directly but that is *implied*, or suggested, by the facts that are given.

Below are five statements that are judgments or ideas that have been arrived at from the facts of the story. Write the letter *C* in the box in front of each statement that is a correct inference. Write the letter *F* in front of each faulty inference.

C—Correct Inference   F—Faulty Inference

- ___ ☐ 1. Daniel Sullivan was probably not as great a hero as he told people he was.
- ___ ☐ 2. If Chicago had had concrete sidewalks, the fire may not have spread as fast.
- ___ ☐ 3. Jeweler A. H. Miller was not a very practical man.
- ___ ☐ 4. Whoever designed the "fireproof" waterworks probably didn't expect a fire to start on the ceiling.
- ___ ☐ 5. The people who sold souvenir hooves of Mrs. O'Leary's cow were swindlers.

Score 5 points for each correct answer

___ TOTAL SCORE: Making Inferences

D USING WORDS PRECISELY

Each of the numbered sentences below contains an underlined word or phrase from the story you have just read. Under the sentence are three definitions. One is a *synonym,* a word that means the same or almost the same thing: *big* and *large.* One is an *antonym,* a word that has the opposite or nearly opposite meaning: *love* and *hate.* One is an unrelated word; it has a completely *different* meaning. Match the definitions with the three answer choices by writing the letter that stands for each answer in the box in front of the definition it goes with.

S—Synonym   A—Antonym   D—Different

1. The store was already underline{smoldering}.

____ ☐ a. burning slowly without flame

____ ☐ b. burning out of control

____ ☐ c. holding back anger

2. The screaming mother pursued the thief as he cut in and out among the crowd. . . .

____ ☐ a. avoided

____ ☐ b. chased

____ ☐ c. sued

3. The mother climbed down the bridge's steelwork and retrieved her infant.

____ ☐ a. recovered

____ ☐ c. lost

____ ☐ c. revived

4. Chicagoans turned their wrath on Patrick O'Leary.

____ ☐ a. punishment

____ ☐ b. rage

____ ☐ c. affection

5. O'Leary hid at a friend's house until the mob's anger died.

____ ☐ a. disorderly crowd

____ ☐ b. herd of animals

____ ☐ c. well-behaved crowd

____ Score 3 points for each correct *S* answer
____ Score 1 point for each correct *A* or *D* answer

____ TOTAL SCORE: Using Words Precisely

● *Enter the four total scores in the spaces below, and add them together to find your Critical Reading Score. Then record your Critical Reading Score on the graph on page 157.*

_____	Finding the Main Idea
_____	Recalling Facts
_____	Making Inferences
_____	Using Words Precisely
_____	CRITICAL READING SCORE: Unit 16

The **Lusitania,** *seen here in port, was an admired British luxury liner often traveled by United States citizens. Despite warnings from Germany, 197 Americans boarded the* **Lusitania** *on its last fateful journey. They should have heeded the warnings! A German submarine attacked the liner in British waters. A total of 1,198 people, more than 100 of them United States citizens, went down with the ship. Who is to blame for their deaths? the Germans? the British? or the victims themselves?*

The Sinking of the *Lusitania*

It had been a good war cruise for German navy officer Walter Schwieger and the crew of his U-boat. The *U-20* had already sunk three British ships and had only two torpedoes left. Now Schwieger had the biggest prize of all in the cross hairs of his periscope—a huge luxury liner. Lieutenant Schwieger carefully checked the angle for a torpedo shot. He then gave the order, "Fire!"

The torpedo ran straight and true. Aboard the large ship, a passenger watched in disbelief as the torpedo approached, churning the water in front of it. As the foaming white feather bore in on the liner, the passenger turned to the next person and asked, "Is that a torpedo?"

A crew member on watch didn't have to wonder what the approaching string of air bubbles meant. The sailor called, "Torpedo coming in on starboard side!"

There was an explosion like the sound of a steel door slamming shut as the torpedo plowed into the *Lusitania*'s Number 1 and Number 2 boilers. Two minutes later, there was a second explosion. This one sounded like a dull thud. The *Lusitania* listed to starboard and began to sink by the head.

Lieutenant Schwieger did not know that the ship he had just fired on was the *Lusitania*. Schwieger did know that he was operating in British waters. And he knew

that British warships might attack at any minute. He felt he had time for just one quick look-around before British rescue ships would begin to arrive. Schwieger ran up his periscope. He made out the name on the now-sinking ship, then quickly gave orders to dive and head for Germany. Later, Schwieger described to his fellow officers the sight of the sinking ship. "The scene was too horrible to watch," he said.

That horrible scene on May 7, 1915, was the death of 1,198 of the 1,918 people aboard the *Lusitania*.

The *Lusitania*'s torpedoing did not come as a complete surprise to its captain or passengers. World War I had been raging for a year. Germany had announced that it intended to carry on unrestricted submarine warfare. It claimed the right to destroy any British ship carrying war supplies to Britain. In fact, shortly before the *Lusitania* sailed, New York newspapers had carried a German advertisement warning United States citizens of the danger of sailing on British ships. The ad was signed and paid for by the Imperial German Embassy in Washington, D.C. It warned its readers not to enter the war zone aboard a British ship.

Despite the ad, 197 United States citizens boarded the *Lusitania* in New York City for a trip to Liverpool, England. For many years, people from the United States had been in

the habit of traveling aboard British ships. They didn't intend to stop because of the World War. The United States wasn't involved in that war. Besides, the *Lusitania* was strictly a passenger ship. Surely, United States citizens reasoned, the Germans wouldn't sink a ship that had hundreds of women and children aboard, and did not carry war cargo.

Captain Will Turner of the *Lusitania* had reason to believe that the Germans might strike, however. He had just received a wireless message from the British Admiralty. The cable stated, "Submarines active off the coast of Ireland." The message failed to indicate just how active the subs were. In the 6 days since the *Lusitania* had sailed from New York, German U-boats had sunk 23 ships near the Irish coast.

Captain Turner ordered the lifeboats made ready, but there was little else that he could do. Will Turner was a perfect sea captain. He had first gone to sea as a 13-year-old cabin boy. He had worked his way up through the ranks to command the world's finest passenger ship.

After the torpedo struck, Captain Turner waited and made certain that there was no chance to save his vessel before giving it up. Then he gave the two ancient calls of the sea: "Abandon ship," and then, "Women and children first!"

Not all of the *Lusitania*'s crew were experienced at sea. Many of them were new to both the ship and to the sea. A large part of the *Lusitania*'s regular crew were members of the naval reserve. They had been called to active warship service at the start of the war. The inexperienced sailors were having real trouble. The steep angle of the *Lusitania*'s list made it difficult for the crew to get the boats into the water. Only one lifeboat out of every eight that the *Lusitania* carried reached shore. A total of 1,198 people died. Of these, 94 were children. Of the 197 people from the United States aboard the *Lusitania,* 128 lost their lives.

Britain branded the *Lusitania*'s sinking a savage act. Germany claimed that it was fighting for its life. The German government stated that it was necessary to sink British ships that were supplying Britain with war goods. Britain, of course, denied that the *Lusitania* carried any war cargo. The United States, which was neutral at the time, treated the taking of American lives as an unforgivable outrage. An adviser to the president, commenting on the *Lusitania*'s sinking, stated, "War with Germany is inevitable." The inevitable came in less than two years. The sinking of the *Lusitania*

was, perhaps, the single most important event leading the United States to enter World War I.

Was the *Lusitania* carrying war goods as Germany claimed? Had the U-boat fired two torpedoes as the British maintained? Or had the second explosion aboard the *Lusitania* been the sound of munitions blowing up? It seemed for years that the answers would lie forever under 250 feet of water. Then in 1950, 35 years after the *Lusitania* went down, the British government released a list of the cargo carried by the great liner. The list showed, quite clearly, that the *Lusitania*'s cargo included cartridges and other war material. ∎

If you have been timed while reading this selection, enter your reading time below. Then turn to the Words-per-Minute table on page 155 and look up your reading speed (words per minute). Enter your reading speed on the graph on page 156.

READING TIME: Unit 17

_____ : _____
Minutes   Seconds

These passengers were among the survivors of the **Lusitania** *tragedy.*

How well did you read?

- *Answer the four types of questions that follow. The directions for each type of question tell you how to mark your answers.*

- *When you have finished all four exercises, check your work by using the answer key on page 152. For each right answer, put a check mark (✓) on the line beside the box. For each wrong answer, write the correct answer on the line.*

- *For scoring each exercise, follow the directions below the questions.*

A FINDING THE MAIN IDEA

Look at the three statements below. One expresses the main idea of the story you just read. A good main idea statement answers two questions: it tells *who* or *what* is the subject of the story, and it answers the understood question *does what?* or *is what?* Another statement is *too broad;* it is vague and doesn't tell much about the topic of the story. The third statement is *too narrow;* it tells about only one part of the story.

Match the statements with the three answer choices below by writing the letter of each answer in the box in front of the statement it goes with.

M—Main Idea   **B—Too Broad**   **N—Too Narrow**

____ ☐ 1. German U-boats operating off the Irish coast sank 24 ships in 6 days.

____ ☐ 2. The sinking of a ship was an important event in World War I.

____ ☐ 3. Many passengers, United States citizens among them, lost their lives when a U-boat sank the *Lusitania.*

____ Score 15 points for a correct *M* answer

____ Score 5 points for each correct *B* or *N* answer

____ TOTAL SCORE: Finding the Main Idea

B RECALLING FACTS

How well do you remember the facts in the story you just read? Put an *x* in the box in front of the correct answer to each of the multiple-choice questions below.

1. Lieutenant Schwieger
   - ____ ☐ a. knew that the ship he fired on was the *Lusitania*.
   - ____ ☐ b. had been hunting the *Lusitania* with his last two torpedoes.
   - ____ ☐ c. only knew that he attacked a ship in British waters.

2. The *Lusitania*'s crew consisted of
   - ____ ☐ a. experienced sailors.
   - ____ ☐ b. many people new to the sea and new to the *Lusitania*.
   - ____ ☐ c. many people new to the ship.

3. The claim that the *Lusitania* had been carrying munitions
   - ____ ☐ a. was found to be true many years after World War I.
   - ____ ☐ b. will probably never be determined.
   - ____ ☐ c. was German propaganda.

4. Lieutenant Schwieger didn't help the *Lusitania* passengers because he
   - ____ ☐ a. wanted to kill as many people as he could.
   - ____ ☐ b. knew British warships would soon attack.
   - ____ ☐ c. knew he couldn't save them all.

5. United States citizens aboard the *Lusitania* should have expected danger because Germany
   - ____ ☐ a. had placed a warning in New York newspapers.
   - ____ ☐ b. had already sunk many ships.
   - ____ ☐ c. was at war with the United States.

Score 5 points for each correct answer

____ TOTAL SCORE: Recalling Facts

C MAKING INFERENCES

An inference is a judgment that is made or an idea that is arrived at based on facts or on information that is given. You make an inference when you understand something that is *not* stated directly but that is *implied*, or suggested, by the facts that are given.

Below are five statements that are judgments or ideas that have been arrived at from the facts of the story. Write the letter *C* in the box in front of each statement that is a correct inference. Write the letter *F* in front of each faulty inference.

C—Correct Inference   F—Faulty Inference

- ____ ☐ 1. Americans were wrong to assume that the Germans would not attack a ship with women and children aboard.

- ____ ☐ 2. The British claim that the second explosion was caused by a torpedo was accurate.

- ____ ☐ 3. The United States government continued to be friendly with Germany after the sinking.

- ____ ☐ 4. Captain Will Turner took the threat of danger seriously.

- ____ ☐ 5. The German U-boat crew did not see the sinking *Lusitania*.

Score 5 points for each correct answer

____ TOTAL SCORE: Making Inferences

D USING WORDS PRECISELY

Each of the numbered sentences below contains an underlined word or phrase from the story you have just read. Under the sentence are three definitions. One is a *synonym*, a word that means the same or almost the same thing: *big* and *large*. One is an *antonym*, a word that has the opposite or nearly opposite meaning: *love* and *hate*. One is an unrelated word; it has a completely *different* meaning. Match the definitions with the three answer choices by writing the letter that stands for each answer in the box in front of the definition it goes with.

S—Synonym   A—Antonym   D—Different

1. Germany had announced that it intended to carry on unrestricted submarine warfare.

   ____ ☐ a. limited by certain rules

   ____ ☐ b. not bound by any rules

   ____ ☐ c. shortened

2. Britain branded the *Lusitania*'s sinking a savage act.

   ____ ☐ a. labeled as shameful

   ____ ☐ b. covered up

   ____ ☐ c. placed a mark showing ownership

3. The United States, which was neutral at the time, treated the taking of American lives as an unforgivable outrage.

   ____ ☐ a. on neither side

   ____ ☐ b. colorless

   ____ ☐ c. for one side

4. An adviser to the president . . . stated, "War with Germany is inevitable."

   ____ ☐ a. avoidable

   ____ ☐ b. certain to happen

   ____ ☐ c. necessary

5. Or had the second explosion aboard the *Lusitania* been the sound of munitions blowing up?

   ____ ☐ a. peacetime supplies

   ____ ☐ b. equipment

   ____ ☐ c. explosives and ammunition

____ Score 3 points for each correct *S* answer

____ Score 1 point for each correct *A* or *D* answer

____ TOTAL SCORE: Using Words Precisely

● *Enter the four total scores in the spaces below, and add them together to find your Critical Reading Score. Then record your Critical Reading Score on the graph on page 157.*

____ Finding the Main Idea

____ Recalling Facts

____ Making Inferences

____ Using Words Precisely

____ CRITICAL READING SCORE: Unit 17

The New London, Texas, Consolidated School was located in the center of one of the world's richest oil fields. Despite this, the townspeople tried to save money by heating the school with a dangerous, raw natural gas. Money was saved, but the price was high—419 lives! Faulty equipment allowed the odorless, raw gas to fill the entire building. The result was a huge explosion that blew the roof off the school and caused the walls to crumble.

Penny-Pinching Brings Death at the World's Richest School

People in Texas claimed that the New London Consolidated School was the world's wealthiest school. It was located in the midst of the world's richest oil field. The two-story brick building served pupils from kindergarten through grade 12. From the school the students could see a forest of oil wells and derricks. By night, the school was lit by the flare of the extra gas from the wells burning off in the air. This same gas was used to heat the Consolidated School, which had no central heating system. Each of the school's radiators burned the gas known as *wet gas* that came directly from the wells.

The wet gas saved the school the $250 to $300 per month it would have cost to heat the school with the regular household gas that many homes use for cooking and heating. Wet gas, however, has several serious disadvantages. It is very uneven in composition, so any equipment that uses wet gas has to be in perfect running order. Unfortunately, not all the radiators at the Consolidated School were in good order. And because wet gas doesn't have the characteristic smell of regular household gas, its presence is undetectable.

Certainly nobody was aware of the gas building up in every corner of every room of the Consolidated School that late afternoon of March 18, 1937. The school day was already over for almost all the pupils in the elementary grades. Students in grades 7 through 12 still had another quarter of an hour of school. It was only by a stroke of bad luck that any students were in school at all. School officials had considered closing a half hour early so that students could attend a track meet. As it turned out, school was not closed, and 690 students were still in the building when tragedy struck.

At 3:15 P.M. there was a long, rumbling explosion and the New London, Texas, Consolidated School blew up.

The roof lifted, the walls bulged outward, and then the roof came back down on top of tables, desks, chairs, and the students and teachers. A Parent Teacher Association meeting was being held in a gymnasium located about 300 feet from the main part of the school. At the sound of the explosion, the mothers ran toward the main building. The first mothers to rush outside saw bodies flying upward through the air. As the mothers looked on in horror, the bodies fell back into the wreckage of what had once been a school.

There were joyous reunions of mothers and the students who had escaped the blast. Then, all the mothers attacked the wreckage, clawing at it with their bare hands. Hundreds of workers from the nearby oil fields joined the mothers. They lifted bricks and beams and plaster in response to moans from underneath the wreckage. After a while, the rescuers had to slow down their frenzied digging. They were afraid of loosening debris that would drop onto the trapped students.

The rescue operation proceeded rapidly but carefully under huge floodlights set up by the oil field workers. A total of 3,000 oil workers used the tools of their trade—acetylene cutting torches and heavy steel cables attached to huge trucks and tractors—to clear away the wreckage. Many of the rescuers were working to save their own children. Eighty-five students were freed from the wreckage alive—though two of them died later. Some of the survivors owed their lives to school desks that protected them from falling debris. One student just happened to be bent over, looking for something under her desk, when the roof and walls collapsed. The desk held, allowing rescuers to save her. Another group of survivors owed their lives to a large bookcase that fell against a wall, forming a tunnel that held until rescue workers dug the students out.

One of every three young people of New London, Texas, died in the explosion. There were 92 seniors in the graduating high school class. Only one survived. In all, 419 bodies were removed from the school.

The people of New London sought to

learn what caused the tragedy, setting up a board of inquiry to sift through the evidence. The board discovered that only one radiator of the six that survived the blast was in working order. This led the investigators to conclude that many of the school's radiators had been leaking wet gas. A great deal of the gas must have built up in an industrial arts shop. The gas needed only one spark to set it off. That spark came when a shop teacher flicked a wall switch to turn on a machine for a student. (It is not known whether that student was one of those who survived.)

Included in the wreckage of the school was a blackboard on which a teacher had written: *Oil and gas are East Texas's greatest mineral blessings. Without them, this school would not be here and none of us would be learning our lessons.* ■

If you have been timed while reading this selection, enter your reading time below. Then turn to the Words-per-Minute table on page 155 and look up your reading speed (words per minute). Enter your reading speed on the graph on page 156.

```
┌─────────────────────────────────────┐
│ READING TIME:  Unit 18               │
│                                      │
│  _____  :  _____         │
│  Minutes          Seconds            │
└─────────────────────────────────────┘
```

How well did you read?

- *Answer the four types of questions that follow. The directions for each type of question tell you how to mark your answers.*

- *When you have finished all four exercises, check your work by using the answer key on page 152. For each right answer, put a check mark (✓) on the line beside the box. For each wrong answer, write the correct answer on the line.*

- *For scoring each exercise, follow the directions below the questions.*

A FINDING THE MAIN IDEA

Look at the three statements below. One expresses the main idea of the story you just read. A good main idea statement answers two questions: it tells *who* or *what* is the subject of the story, and it answers the understood question *does what?* or *is what?* Another statement is *too broad;* it is vague and doesn't tell much about the topic of the story. The third statement is *too narrow;* it tells about only one part of the story.

Match the statements with the three answer choices below by writing the letter of each answer in the box in front of the statement it goes with.

M—Main Idea   **B—Too Broad**   **N—Too Narrow**

_____ ☐ 1. A deadly gas explosion tore apart a Texas school, killing 419 children.

_____ ☐ 2. No one was aware of the dangerous conditions at the Consolidated School.

_____ ☐ 3. Many oil field workers tried to free their own children from the Consolidated School wreckage.

_____ Score 15 points for a correct *M* answer

_____ Score 5 points for each correct *B* or *N* answer

_____ TOTAL SCORE: Finding the Main Idea

B RECALLING FACTS

How well do you remember the facts in the story you just read? Put an *x* in the box in front of the correct answer to each of the multiple-choice questions below.

1. Wet gas
   - ____ ☐ a. is ordinarily safer to burn than regular household gas.
   - ____ ☐ b. requires that radiators be in perfect condition.
   - ____ ☐ c. is manufactured from regular household gas.

2. Workers slowed down their rescue efforts because they
   - ____ ☐ a. were afraid more wreckage would fall on top of the trapped pupils.
   - ____ ☐ b. couldn't see much after the sun went down.
   - ____ ☐ c. were tired after an afternoon and evening of digging.

3. The explosion probably started in
   - ____ ☐ a. a chemistry laboratory.
   - ____ ☐ b. the school's kitchen.
   - ____ ☐ c. an industrial arts shop.

4. The Consolidated School was located in
   - ____ ☐ a. Lubbock, Texas.
   - ____ ☐ b. New London, Texas.
   - ____ ☐ c. Dallas, Texas.

5. The oil field workers used
   - ____ ☐ a. the tools of their trade in their rescue attempts.
   - ____ ☐ b. their bare hands.
   - ____ ☐ c. special cranes and torches designed for rescue work.

Score 5 points for each correct answer

____ TOTAL SCORE: Recalling Facts

C MAKING INFERENCES

An inference is a judgment that is made or an idea that is arrived at based on facts or on information that is given. You make an inference when you understand something that is *not* stated directly but that is *implied*, or suggested, by the facts that are given.

Below are five statements that are judgments or ideas that have been arrived at from the facts of the story. Write the letter *C* in the box in front of each statement that is a correct inference. Write the letter *F* in front of each faulty inference.

C—Correct Inference   F—Faulty Inference

- ____ ☐ 1. School officials in New London were not very thrifty.
- ____ ☐ 2. Almost all the school-aged children of New London, Texas, died in the explosion.
- ____ ☐ 3. The first people on the scene were PTA mothers.
- ____ ☐ 4. More people took part in the rescue work than the number of pupils attending the school.
- ____ ☐ 5. The cause of the explosion was probably one or more faulty radiators.

Score 5 points for each correct answer

____ TOTAL SCORE: Making Inferences

D USING WORDS PRECISELY

Each of the numbered sentences below contains an underlined word or phrase from the story you have just read. Under the sentence are three definitions. One is a *synonym*, a word that means the same or almost the same thing: *big* and *large*. One is an *antonym*, a word that has the opposite or nearly opposite meaning: *love* and *hate*. One is an unrelated word; it has a completely *different* meaning. Match the definitions with the three answer choices by writing the letter that stands for each answer in the box in front of the definition it goes with.

S—Synonym   A—Antonym   D—Different

1. Wet gas is very <u>uneven in composition</u>. . . .

____ ☐ a. the same throughout

____ ☐ b. not written well

____ ☐ c. varying in makeup

2. And because wet gas doesn't have the <u>characteristic</u> smell of regular household gas, . . .

____ ☐ a. typical

____ ☐ b. irregular

____ ☐ c. playing a role

3. After a while, the rescuers had to slow down their <u>frenzied</u> digging.

____ ☐ a. wildly excited

____ ☐ b. disorderly

____ ☐ c. relaxed

4. They were afraid of loosening <u>debris</u> that would drop onto the trapped students.

____ ☐ a. pieces of junk

____ ☐ b. solid, valuable material

____ ☐ c. recycled trash

5. The people . . . sought to learn what caused the tragedy, setting up a <u>board of inquiry</u> to sift through the evidence.

____ ☐ a. group of school administrators

____ ☐ b. group seeking clues

____ ☐ c. people hiding evidence

____ Score 3 points for each correct *S* answer

____ Score 1 point for each correct *A* or *D* answer

____ **TOTAL SCORE:** Using Words Precisely

● *Enter the four total scores in the spaces below, and add them together to find your Critical Reading Score. Then record your Critical Reading Score on the graph on page 157.*

_____ Finding the Main Idea

_____ Recalling Facts

_____ Making Inferences

_____ Using Words Precisely

_____ **CRITICAL READING SCORE:** Unit 18

After the nuclear explosion at Chernobyl in 1986, helicopters circled the power station day and night monitoring radiation levels. The worst nuclear accident in history put the lives of thousands of people in danger. By 1991 one expert on Chernobyl said that at least 7,000 people had died from radiation exposure. These two children were among those exposed.

Atomic Meltdown at Chernobyl

At a nuclear power plant in Sweden one Monday morning, a worker walked past a radiation detector and set off the dreaded alarm. Officials quickly checked his clothing and were shocked to find dangerously high levels of radiation. Fearing a deadly radiation leak, officials evacuated the plant. They tested all 600 employees to determine if they, too, were "hot"—and they were! Officials then tested the ground and the bushes around the power station and found five times the normal level of radiation. But inside the plant, there was nothing wrong. What was going on?

The Swedes alerted the United States when other power stations around the country also reported high radiation levels. Soon reports of radiation poured in from Finland, Norway, and Denmark. Although the Swedes were relieved that the source of radiation was not their own country, they wanted to know where it was coming from. Had there been a nuclear explosion somewhere?

By Monday afternoon, April 28, 1986, Swedish officials had figured out that the atomic fallout was being carried by the wind. Scientists studied the radioactive material and the wind pattern and concluded that a nuclear accident had indeed occurred. They tracked the radioactive cloud to the Ukraine, a republic in the former Soviet Union.

A Swedish diplomat in Moscow, meanwhile, began to ask probing questions. But for 12 hours there was no reply from the Soviet government. Even the Soviet people were kept in the dark. Finally, at 9 P.M., the Soviets announced that there had been a nuclear reactor accident at the Chernobyl power plant. No casualties or other details on the worst nuclear accident in history were reported that night. The Soviets also kept secret that the explosion had happened three full days before.

From satellite photographs, scientists in the United States viewed the Chernobyl disaster. An explosion had blown the roof off a huge atomic reactor. Walls around the reactor bulged out, and in the center of the wreckage, a white hot fire was blazing.

Chernobyl is located 80 miles north of Kiev, the capital of the Ukraine. The nuclear facility was old and poorly built. Inside its reactors were graphite bricks that could stop or slow down the nuclear chain reaction. Graphite, a form of carbon, was used to absorb radiation. But graphite is dangerous. If it catches fire, it can reach temperatures of more than 5,000 degrees Celsius. Because of this, most modern nuclear power plants no longer use graphite reactors. And they reinforce the buildings that house their atomic reactors with a concrete shell. The shell is designed to prevent radioactive materials from escaping during an accident. Chernobyl did not have this safety device. So when one of its reactors exploded and the graphite ignited, radioactive debris escaped freely into the air.

The Soviets moved quickly but quietly shortly after the accident. They sealed off the power plant and started to evacuate residents who lived within 19 miles of the facility. Some 50,000 people had to leave all their belongings behind and board buses and trains that would take them away from Chernobyl. Medical teams, scientists, and other experts arrived at the scene. Doctors were shocked to find people whose skin had turned brown. Their hair and eyelashes had fallen out. They felt weak and sick. One man said when he got out of his bed and stood up, the skin on his leg slipped off as if it had been a stocking. Some victims were so "hot" that even the doctors treating them became dangerously exposed.

The situation at Chernobyl worsened each day, yet the Soviets said little and asked for little from the outside world. They desperately tried to put out the raging graphite fire at the plant. Huge helicopters were brought in to attack the fire from the air. To protect the pilots from radiation, sheets of lead were placed under their seats. The brave pilots repeatedly flew over the reactor and dropped clay, lead, sand, and other materials on the inferno. They did not use water because it would have only fueled the flames. It took more than 5,000 tons of materials and 12 days to put out the fire. When ground crews could get near the plant, they bore tunnels under the concrete slab that supported the reactor. Water was then pumped into the tunnels to lower the temperature of the burning reactor core.

The area around Chernobyl remained "hot" for months after the accident. Work crews had to limit the time they spent near the reactor, so the cleanup took longer. There was so much contaminated soil that the government didn't know where to bury it all. As for the damaged reactor, officials decided to encase it in a gigantic coffin. Trucks carrying ready-mix cement poured it into specially made steel vats. The cement-filled vats were like bricks. They formed a concrete wall, the "coffin," around the reactor.

The cleanup and safety measures taken by the Soviets did little to satisfy the rest of the world. The radioactive fallout had covered large sections of the Ukraine and other parts of the former Soviet Union before spreading across most of Europe. Europeans were outraged. They accepted that the nuclear blast had been an accident, but they were furious that the Soviets tried to hide what happened. They were denied the chance to protect themselves.

Radioactive fallout contaminated water, land, livestock, and food supplies. Poland, which had radiation levels as high as 100,000 times the normal level, feared for the lives of its children. People were told not to eat farm products or drink milk from cows. In Norway, Sweden, and Finland, people were told not to drink or use rain water or eat freshwater fish. Officials in Italy banned the sales of some food because they were "hot." In Scotland farmers could not sell the meat from their sheep because the animals had grazed on contaminated grass.

The Soviets claimed that only 31 people died because of Chernobyl, but the actual number is much higher. Since the accident, countless new cases of cancer have developed. Scientists estimate that perhaps more victims may die from the Chernobyl blast than all the people killed in World War II. And many areas affected by Chernobyl will remain "hot" for thousands of years, too "hot" to sustain life. ∎

If you have been timed while reading this selection, enter your reading time below. Then turn to the Words-per-Minute table on page 155 and look up your reading speed (words per minute). Enter your reading speed on the graph on page 156.

READING TIME: Unit 19

_____ : _____
Minutes   Seconds

How well did you read?

- *Answer the four types of questions that follow. The directions for each type of question tell you how to mark your answers.*

- *When you have finished all four exercises, check your work by using the answer key on page 152. For each right answer, put a check mark (✓) on the line beside the box. For each wrong answer, write the correct answer on the line.*

- *For scoring each exercise, follow the directions below the questions.*

A FINDING THE MAIN IDEA

Look at the three statements below. One expresses the main idea of the story you just read. A good main idea statement answers two questions: it tells *who* or *what* is the subject of the story, and it answers the understood question *does what?* or *is what?* Another statement is *too broad;* it is vague and doesn't tell much about the topic of the story. The third statement is *too narrow;* it tells about only one part of the story.

Match the statements with the three answer choices below by writing the letter of each answer in the box in front of the statement it goes with.

M—Main Idea   **B—Too Broad**   **N—Too Narrow**

_____ ☐ 1. A nuclear explosion resulted in widespread contamination.

_____ ☐ 2. The Soviet Union tried to hide from the world what happened at Chernobyl.

_____ ☐ 3. Thirty-one people died as a direct result of the Chernobyl blast.

_____ Score 15 points for a correct *M* answer

_____ Score 5 points for each correct *B* or *N* answer

_____ TOTAL SCORE: Finding the Main Idea

B RECALLING FACTS

How well do you remember the facts in the story you just read? Put an *x* in the box in front of the correct answer to each of the multiple-choice questions below.

1. High radiation levels were first noticed by
   - ___ ☐ a. Russia.
   - ___ ☐ b. Sweden.
   - ___ ☐ c. a United States satellite.

2. Chernobyl is located north of
   - ___ ☐ a. the Ukraine.
   - ___ ☐ b. Kiev.
   - ___ ☐ c. the capital of Russia.

3. Most modern nuclear reactors
   - ___ ☐ a. have at least one major accident.
   - ___ ☐ b. are surrounded by a protective shell.
   - ___ ☐ c. operate without any risks.

4. Many European countries
   - ___ ☐ a. were seriously affected by the radiation.
   - ___ ☐ b. sympathized with the Soviets.
   - ___ ☐ c. were unharmed by the radiation.

5. In an attempt to contain the radiation, Soviet officials decided to
   - ___ ☐ a. flood the reactor.
   - ___ ☐ b. move the reactor to an uninhabited area.
   - ___ ☐ c. enclose the reactor in a concrete coffin.

Score 5 points for each correct answer

___ TOTAL SCORE: Recalling Facts

C MAKING INFERENCES

An inference is a judgment that is made or an idea that is arrived at based on facts or on information that is given. You make an inference when you understand something that is *not* stated directly but that is *implied,* or suggested, by the facts that are given.

Below are five statements that are judgments or ideas that have been arrived at from the facts of the story. Write the letter *C* in the box in front of each statement that is a correct inference. Write the letter *F* in front of each faulty inference.

C—Correct Inference   F—Faulty Inference

- ___ ☐ 1. At the time of the accident, not much was known about nuclear power.
- ___ ☐ 2. Soviet nuclear reactors are safer than American reactors.
- ___ ☐ 3. Swedish officials feared a serious radiation leak at one of their nuclear plants.
- ___ ☐ 4. Norway and Finland reported the highest levels of radioactive fallout.
- ___ ☐ 5. The Soviets were capable of handling the disaster by themselves.

Score 5 points for each correct answer

___ TOTAL SCORE: Making Inferences

D USING WORDS PRECISELY

Each of the numbered sentences below contains an underlined word or phrase from the story you have just read. Under the sentence are three definitions. One is a *synonym*, a word that means the same or almost the same thing: *big* and *large*. One is an *antonym*, a word that has the opposite or nearly opposite meaning: *love* and *hate*. One is an unrelated word; it has a completely *different* meaning. Match the definitions with the three answer choices by writing the letter that stands for each answer in the box in front of the definition it goes with.

S—Synonym   A—Antonym   D—Different

1. Fearing a deadly <u>radiation</u> leak, officials evacuated the plant.

____ ☐ a. intense heat

____ ☐ b. nuclear activity

____ ☐ c. harmless gases

2. A Swedish diplomat in Moscow, meanwhile, began to ask <u>probing</u> questions.

____ ☐ a. vague and unclear

____ ☐ b. experimental

____ ☐ c. intelligent and important

3. The radioactive <u>fallout</u> had covered large sections of the Ukraine and other parts of the Soviet Union. . . .

____ ☐ a. heavy downpour

____ ☐ b. dust from a nuclear explosion

____ ☐ c. disagreement

4. Europeans were <u>outraged</u>.

____ ☐ a. very angry

____ ☐ b. extremely happy

____ ☐ c. insulted

5. And many areas affected by Chernobyl will remain . . . too "hot" to <u>sustain</u> life.

____ ☐ a. support and maintain

____ ☐ b. weaken

____ ☐ c. confirm

____ Score 3 points for each correct *S* answer
____ Score 1 point for each correct *A* or *D* answer

____ TOTAL SCORE: Using Words Precisely

● *Enter the four total scores in the spaces below, and add them together to find your Critical Reading Score. Then record your Critical Reading Score on the graph on page 157.*

____ Finding the Main Idea
____ Recalling Facts
____ Making Inferences
____ Using Words Precisely
____ CRITICAL READING SCORE: Unit 19

The year was 1906. The people of San Francisco were very proud of their modern, trendy city. But a sudden jolt from a powerful earthquake and raging fires quickly changed this beloved city to ruin. On many San Francisco streets, residents gazed in amazement at the widespread destruction. Their homes had been destroyed, and they had nowhere else to go.

The San Francisco Earthquake

On April 18, 1906, at 5:12 A.M., San Francisco was rocked by a great earthquake. Although the quake itself lasted just seconds, it was indirectly responsible for the destruction of three-fourths of the entire city. About 300,000 people were made homeless, and 38,000 buildings were destroyed.

The earthquake itself caused little of this damage. The principal destructive force was the fire caused by the quake. Survivors of the San Francisco disaster have always referred to it, not as "the Earthquake of 1906" but as "the Great Fire of 1906."

San Francisco was a very modern city in 1906, and its modern power system was responsible for its destruction. The shock of the quake broke petroleum tanks, and the upheaval of the streets snapped gas mains. All the situation needed to set off a giant conflagration was one spark, and there were sparks aplenty from the broken overhead electric wires. Within seconds, a large part of the city was on fire.

Unfortunately, one of the victims of the quake was the head of the city's fire department. He was crushed to death when the chimney of his home fell on top of him.

The fire department was handicapped not only by the tragic loss of its leader but also by the loss of almost all of its water supply. The tremor had snapped the water mains buried deep in the ground. Moreover, the quake had destroyed the city's fire alarm boxes and all telephone communications.

Even if the fire fighters could have received orders, it would have been difficult for them to report to their firehouses since travel, including public transportation, had been brought to a standstill. Train and streetcar lines suffered twisted rails from the upheaval of the streets. During the first few hours after the quake, individual fire fighters and small fire companies could do little more than help extricate victims who were lying helpless, pinned under the wreckage of collapsed buildings.

All civil authorities were as handicapped as the fire department. However, a large military post was located in San Francisco. General Frederick Funston, United States Army, commanded the troops in San Francisco. As a young man Funston had tried to get into West Point but had failed the Military Academy's entrance exam. He enlisted in the army as a private, and his heroism brought him rapid promotion. During service in the Philippine Islands, he won the Congressional Medal of Honor, the highest award the United States gives for valor.

Now, with the city in flames, and the police and fire departments overwhelmed, General Funston took charge. He placed the city under martial law and ordered his troops into the streets. The soldiers carried loaded rifles with bayonets and had orders to "shoot to kill" to prevent looting. Many people had been forced to flee from their homes with only the clothes on their backs. These refugees, in their haste and confusion, had abandoned their homes and valuables, often without even remaining behind long enough to lock their doors. The troops were assigned to protect homes from roving bands of robbers.

The troops' second assignment was to use dynamite and artillery to blow up buildings in the line of the fire's advance. This would create firebreaks, flat areas in the path of the fire that would halt its advance by denying it any fuel on which it could feed. Some of the firebreaks did work to slow down the spread of the conflagration. Often, however, before the troops could detonate the dynamite they had planted, the rapidly advancing blaze set it off. The premature explosions hurled flaming wreckage onto buildings not yet touched by the flames. Thus, the dynamiting, rather than retarding the advance of the blaze, sometimes spread it to new areas.

The troops' other mission, the prevention of looting, accomplished a great deal of good, but it also did some harm. The presence of armed soldiers did discourage some would-be looters, but the troops also shot or bayoneted some innocent citizens who were trying to remove their own valuables from their homes before the flames reached them. There is also some evidence that a few soldiers actually became looters themselves, stealing the very property that they were supposed to be guarding.

One section of the city that did not fall victim to either the fire or the dynamiters was the area known as Telegraph Hill. The Italian families who lived there fought the fire block by block and house by house. They fought with brooms and blankets and buckets of water from San Francisco Bay. And when there was no water, they fought with barrels of homemade red wine from their cellars. They fought—and they won.

Three days after the earthquake, the flames began to come under control. As the blaze approached the waterfront, the city's fire fighters, aided by forces from nearby cities, were able to draw water from San Francisco Bay. Their efforts, combined with a shift in wind direction, finally brought the flames under control.

Three-fourths of the city had been destroyed by the quake and the fires that followed. About 700 people had lost their lives, and many of the people who survived felt that they had been touched by God— and spared.

Within five years after the earthquake, San Francisco had been rebuilt and showed no signs of the destruction left by the quake or the fire. Today, San Francisco is one of the largest cities in the United States. And its residents know all about the danger of earthquakes. In 1989 the strongest quake since 1906 hit the Bay Area, killing 55 people and causing billions of dollars worth of damage. ∎

If you have been timed while reading this selection, enter your reading time below. Then turn to the Words-per-Minute table on page 155 and look up your reading speed (words per minute). Enter your reading speed on the graph on page 156.

READING TIME: Unit 20

_____ : _____
Minutes   *Seconds*

How well did you read?

- *Answer the four types of questions that follow. The directions for each type of question tell you how to mark your answers.*

- *When you have finished all four exercises, check your work by using the answer key on page 152. For each right answer, put a check mark (✓) on the line beside the box. For each wrong answer, write the correct answer on the line.*

- *For scoring each exercise, follow the directions below the questions.*

A   FINDING THE MAIN IDEA

Look at the three statements below. One expresses the main idea of the story you just read. A good main idea statement answers two questions: it tells *who* or *what* is the subject of the story, and it answers the understood question *does what?* or *is what?* Another statement is *too broad;* it is vague and doesn't tell much about the topic of the story. The third statement is *too narrow;* it tells about only one part of the story.

Match the statements with the three answer choices below by writing the letter of each answer in the box in front of the statement it goes with.

M—Main Idea   B—Too Broad   N—Too Narrow

_____ ☐ 1. Earthquakes and fires can be a deadly combination.

_____ ☐ 2. Broken power and gas lines set off fires throughout San Francisco.

_____ ☐ 3. The fires caused by the San Francisco earthquake were even more destructive than the quake itself.

_____ Score 15 points for a correct *M* answer

_____ Score 5 points for each correct *B* or *N* answer

_____ TOTAL SCORE: Finding the Main Idea

139

B RECALLING FACTS

How well do you remember the facts in the story you just read? Put an *x* in the box in front of the correct answer to each of the multiple-choice questions below.

1. After the quake streetcars were not running because the
   - ___ ☐ a. motormen who were supposed to drive them did not show up for work.
   - ___ ☐ b. tracks were twisted.
   - ___ ☐ c. the general ordered them shut down.

2. The fire department was hampered by
   - ___ ☐ a. interference from the soldiers.
   - ___ ☐ b. lack of water.
   - ___ ☐ c. homeowners who feared the fire fighters would loot their houses.

3. Dynamiting buildings
   - ___ ☐ a. sometimes resulted in spreading the fire.
   - ___ ☐ b. was responsible for saving many parts of the city.
   - ___ ☐ c. prevented looting.

4. The quake and the resulting fires left
   - ___ ☐ a. 3,000 people homeless.
   - ___ ☐ b. 38,000 people homeless.
   - ___ ☐ c. 300,000 people homeless.

5. When the Italian families who lived on Telegraph Hill ran out of water, they
   - ___ ☐ a. stopped fighting the fire and fled for their lives.
   - ___ ☐ b. used homemade wine.
   - ___ ☐ c. got more water from San Francisco Bay.

Score 5 points for each correct answer

___ TOTAL SCORE: Recalling Facts

C MAKING INFERENCES

An inference is a judgment that is made or an idea that is arrived at based on facts or on information that is given. You make an inference when you understand something that is *not* stated directly but that is *implied*, or suggested, by the facts that are given.

Below are five statements that are judgments or ideas that have been arrived at from the facts of the story. Write the letter *C* in the box in front of each statement that is a correct inference. Write the letter *F* in front of each faulty inference.

C—Correct Inference   F—Faulty Inference

- ___ ☐ 1. It was fortunate that a large military post was located in San Francisco.
- ___ ☐ 2. General Funston was a brave man.
- ___ ☐ 3. The troops called in to prevent looting did more harm than good.
- ___ ☐ 4. The residents of Telegraph Hill showed a tremendous amount of determination.
- ___ ☐ 5. Although many years have passed since the earthquake of 1906, San Francisco has never fully recovered.

Score 5 points for each correct answer

___ TOTAL SCORE: Making Inferences

D USING WORDS PRECISELY

Each of the numbered sentences below contains an underlined word or phrase from the story you have just read. Under the sentence are three definitions. One is a *synonym*, a word that means the same or almost the same thing: *big* and *large*. One is an *antonym*, a word that has the opposite or nearly opposite meaning: *love* and *hate*. One is an unrelated word; it has a completely *different* meaning. Match the definitions with the three answer choices by writing the letter that stands for each answer in the box in front of the definition it goes with.

S—Synonym   A—Antonym   D—Different

1. The shock of the quake broke petroleum tanks, and the underlined upheaval of the streets snapped gas mains.

___ ☐ a. confusion

___ ☐ b. sinking

___ ☐ c. lifting from below

2. . . . fire fighters and small fire companies could do little more than help underlined extricate victims who were lying helpless. . . .

___ ☐ a. tie or pin down

___ ☐ b. free

___ ☐ c. distinguish

3. During service in the Philippine Islands, he [General Funston] won the . . . highest award the United States gives for underlined valor.

___ ☐ a. bravery

___ ☐ b. loyalty

___ ☐ c. cowardice

4. He placed the city under underlined martial law and ordered his troops into the streets.

___ ☐ a. emergency

___ ☐ b. military

___ ☐ c. civilian

5. Thus, the dynamiting, rather than underlined retarding the advance of the blaze, sometimes spread it to new areas.

___ ☐ a. slowing down

___ ☐ b. speeding up

___ ☐ c. blocking

___ Score 3 points for each correct *S* answer
___ Score 1 point for each correct *A* or *D* answer

___ TOTAL SCORE: Using Words Precisely

● *Enter the four total scores in the spaces below, and add them together to find your Critical Reading Score. Then record your Critical Reading Score on the graph on page 157.*

_____	Finding the Main Idea
_____	Recalling Facts
_____	Making Inferences
_____	Using Words Precisely
_____	**CRITICAL READING SCORE: Unit 20**

More than 75 years ago, reporter Ralph Frye was sent out to investigate a possible fire in the North End of Boston. Frye headed toward Commercial Street, expecting to see smoke or flames. He didn't see either. In a quick call to his editor, he said, "This is no fire. I don't know what it is. . . . There seems to be an awful stink of molasses around here." Within minutes a furious sea of gooey molasses came rushing toward him. It was "the story of all stories."

Boston's Great Molasses Flood

Have you ever heard someone described as being "slower than molasses in January"? Molasses is a thick, sticky, sugary syrup that moves very slowly when it is poured. And the colder it is, the stickier and slower-moving molasses becomes. But one January afternoon—January 15, 1919—molasses moved so fast that it snuffed out the lives of 21 people and destroyed a large section of Boston's North End.

For nearly three centuries, molasses played a key role in Boston's economy. Colonists used molasses in place of high-priced sugar. They also used the sticky syrup to make and sell their own rum. The community of Boston depended on the trade generated from the sale and manufacture of molasses.

Ironically, the molasses industry was about to suffer a devastating blow that fateful January. Only one more state was needed to approve Prohibition, the 18th Amendment to the United States Constitution, and the vote was certain. Nebraska would make the sale and manufacture of any alcoholic beverage illegal. The passage of Prohibition would spell disaster for the molasses industry. But before the dreaded news from Nebraska could spread across the North End community, Boston's massive molasses tank exploded.

The huge metal tank loomed high above Commercial Street, near Boston's harbor,

supported by a frame of metal legs. The tank itself was 50 feet tall; and it was almost 300 feet (the length of a football field) around. Inside the tank were steam pipes that kept the molasses warm. On January 12, the tank was filled beyond its capacity. It was intended to hold almost 2 million gallons of molasses, but now the tank held more than 2.3 million gallons.

January 15 was an unusually warm day in Boston. At midday people were outdoors enjoying the sunshine. Workers from factories and warehouses were outside on loading docks eating lunch. And many of the North End shopkeepers and residents, newly arrived immigrants from Italy, were standing in doorways. They remarked how the warm weather was reminiscent of their sunny home country.

Suddenly, the balmy day was shattered by a deep rumbling sound . . . then a series of deafening explosions. The molasses tank had burst open! A flood of steaming hot liquid gushed out and poured down Commercial Street. And there was nothing slow about the way *this* molasses ran that January afternoon. People in its path couldn't run fast enough to avoid it. The sludge grabbed their feet and swirled them around. Other people scrambled to keep ahead of the sticky, 30-foot-high wave of molasses, but it was hopeless. Twenty-seven

million pounds of the sticky goo poured over walkers, lunch crowds, and factory workers. It demolished buildings and lifted some right off their foundations. Twenty-one people were either crushed by the wreckage or drowned in the gooey substance in a matter of minutes.

Meanwhile, a northbound train on Boston's new elevated railway was heading straight for disaster. As the train rounded a curve, the brakeman suddenly saw the raging flood of molasses before him. He quickly pulled the emergency cord, and the train stopped, just barely avoiding a deadly plunge into the swirling sea of molasses below. Flying pieces of the broken tank had sliced through the 15-inch supporting shafts of the elevated tracks, toppling them into the savage flood.

Although there were cars and trucks back in the year 1919, most freight was still hauled by horses and wagons. Dozens of carts became trapped in the sticky sludge. Horses reared and snorted, rolling their eyes in terror as they found themselves mired in the ooze. Many of them were bowled over and suffocated. Those horses alive, but trapped in the syrup, were helpless and suffering. Police had to shoot some of the terrified beasts to put them out of their misery.

Many well-meaning bystanders who tried to help the trapped victims soon found themselves snared knee-deep in sticky molasses. The stuff was worse than quicksand. Rescuers had to cut people right out of their clothes in order to free them. The clothes had become crusted with crystallized sugar.

As weary rescuers and residents slowly returned to their homes, they spread the molasses all over the city. The next day every city bench in the area was sticky. Molasses covered buses, trees, roofs, and overhead wires. The cleanup went on for days. Even after the injured had been cared for and the dead had been buried, Boston continued to live a nightmare. It was weeks before the odor of molasses disappeared. And the waters of Boston Harbor had a brown cast for months afterward.

What caused the disaster? Purity Distilling Company, the firm that owned the tank, blamed the collapse on vibrations caused by a passing train. But most people didn't buy that explanation. Later, the company changed its story. It claimed that political anarchists had deliberately caused the explosion. Bostonians didn't buy that story either. Most people simply thought that the warm weather, coming in the midst of January's usual cold, had caused the molasses to heat up, expand, and burst the tank's seams.

There was, of course, an investigation. The official verdict was that the original workmanship of the tank had been shoddy. The tank's owners had to pay heavy damages to the families of victims and to those who lost property. But no amount of money could ever make up for the suffering and loss of 21 lives in what has become known as "Boston's Great Molasses Flood." ∎

If you have been timed while reading this selection, enter your reading time below. Then turn to the Words-per-Minute table on page 155 and look up your reading speed (words per minute). Enter your reading speed on the graph on page 156.

READING TIME: Unit 21

_____ : _____
Minutes   Seconds

How well did you read?

- *Answer the four types of questions that follow. The directions for each type of question tell you how to mark your answers.*

- *When you have finished all four exercises, check your work by using the answer key on page 152. For each right answer, put a check mark (✓) on the line beside the box. For each wrong answer, write the correct answer on the line.*

- *For scoring each exercise, follow the directions below the questions.*

A — FINDING THE MAIN IDEA

Look at the three statements below. One expresses the main idea of the story you just read. A good main idea statement answers two questions: it tells *who* or *what* is the subject of the story, and it answers the understood question *does what?* or *is what?* Another statement is *too broad;* it is vague and doesn't tell much about the topic of the story. The third statement is *too narrow;* it tells about only one part of the story.

Match the statements with the three answer choices below by writing the letter of each answer in the box in front of the statement it goes with.

M — Main Idea   **B — Too Broad**   **N — Too Narrow**

____ ☐ 1. Many innocent people were killed in an accident in Boston's North End community.

____ ☐ 2. Death and destruction occurred after a tank of molasses exploded onto a Boston street.

____ ☐ 3. More than 2 million gallons of molasses raced through the streets of Boston one January afternoon.

____ Score 15 points for a correct *M* answer

____ Score 5 points for each correct *B* or *N* answer

____ TOTAL SCORE: Finding the Main Idea

B RECALLING FACTS

How well do you remember the facts in the story you just read? Put an *x* in the box in front of the correct answer to each of the multiple-choice questions below.

1. The day the tank burst was
   - ____ ☐ a. unusually cold for January.
   - ____ ☐ b. unusually warm for January.
   - ____ ☐ c. very hot and humid.

2. When the tank burst there was
   - ____ ☐ a. no sound.
   - ____ ☐ b. a high, squealing sound.
   - ____ ☐ c. a deep rumbling, then explosions.

3. The passage of Prohibition would have
   - ____ ☐ a. improved Boston's molasses industry.
   - ____ ☐ b. had no effect on Boston's molasses industry.
   - ____ ☐ c. crippled Boston's molasses industry.

4. Well-meaning bystanders
   - ____ ☐ a. became trapped in the gooey molasses.
   - ____ ☐ b. rescued most of the victims.
   - ____ ☐ c. were forced to leave the scene.

5. A northbound train
   - ____ ☐ a. plunged into the molasses below.
   - ____ ☐ b. was swept into the harbor.
   - ____ ☐ c. nearly plunged into the sea of molasses.

Score 5 points for each correct answer

____ TOTAL SCORE: Recalling Facts

C MAKING INFERENCES

An inference is a judgment that is made or an idea that is arrived at based on facts or on information that is given. You make an inference when you understand something that is *not* stated directly but that is *implied*, or suggested, by the facts that are given.

Below are five statements that are judgments or ideas that have been arrived at from the facts of the story. Write the letter C in the box in front of each statement that is a correct inference. Write the letter F in front of each faulty inference.

C—Correct Inference   F—Faulty Inference

- ____ ☐ 1. If the day had been colder more people would have died.
- ____ ☐ 2. Police could have saved the trapped horses.
- ____ ☐ 3. No one had the courage to help those stuck in the molasses.
- ____ ☐ 4. The company that owned the tank was willing to accept responsibility for the accident.
- ____ ☐ 5. The tank had not been well constructed.

Score 5 points for each correct answer

____ TOTAL SCORE: Making Inferences

D USING WORDS PRECISELY

Each of the numbered sentences below contains an underlined word or phrase from the story you have just read. Under the sentence are three definitions. One is a *synonym*, a word that means the same or almost the same thing: *big* and *large*. One is an *antonym*, a word that has the opposite or nearly opposite meaning: *love* and *hate*. One is an unrelated word; it has a completely *different* meaning. Match the definitions with the three answer choices by writing the letter that stands for each answer in the box in front of the definition it goes with.

S—Synonym   A—Antonym   D—Different

1. They remarked how the warm weather was <u>reminiscent</u> of their sunny home country.

   ___ ☐ a. forgotten or neglected

   ___ ☐ b. recalled to mind

   ___ ☐ c. similar to

2. Suddenly, the <u>balmy</u> day was shattered by a deep rumbling sound. . . .

   ___ ☐ a. foolish

   ___ ☐ b. stormy and cold

   ___ ☐ c. mild and pleasant

3. Horses reared and snorted, rolling their eyes in terror as they found themselves <u>mired</u> in the ooze.

   ___ ☐ a. released from

   ___ ☐ b. exhausted

   ___ ☐ c. trapped

4. The clothes had become crusted with <u>crystallized</u> sugar.

   ___ ☐ a. turned from liquid to solid

   ___ ☐ b. melted

   ___ ☐ c. spoiled

5. And the waters of Boston Harbor had a brown <u>cast</u> for months afterward.

   ___ ☐ a. a shading of color

   ___ ☐ b. an expression

   ___ ☐ c. a deep color

   ___ Score 3 points for each correct *S* answer
   ___ Score 1 point for each correct *A* or *D* answer
   ___ TOTAL SCORE: Using Words Precisely

● *Enter the four total scores in the spaces below, and add them together to find your Critical Reading Score. Then record your Critical Reading Score on the graph on page 157.*

   _____ Finding the Main Idea
   _____ Recalling Facts
   _____ Making Inferences
   _____ Using Words Precisely
   _____ CRITICAL READING SCORE: Unit 21

147

ANSWER KEY

1 Emergency on Avianca Flight 52
A. Finding the Main Idea
   1. **M**   2. **N**   3. **B**
B. Recalling Facts
   1. **c**   2. **c**   3. **a**   4. **b**   5. **c**
C. Making Inferences
   1. **C**   2. **C**   3. **C**   4. **C**   5. **F**
D. Using Words Precisely
   1. a. **S**   b. **A**   c. **D**
   2. a. **A**   b. **D**   c. **S**
   3. a. **A**   b. **S**   c. **D**
   4. a. **D**   b. **S**   c. **A**
   5. a. **D**   b. **A**   c. **S**

2 Custer's Last Stand
A. Finding the Main Idea
   1. **M**   2. **B**   3. **N**
B. Recalling Facts
   1. **a**   2. **b**   3. **b**   4. **c**   5. **a**
C. Making Inferences
   1. **C**   2. **C**   3. **F**   4. **F**   5. **C**
D. Using Words Precisely
   1. a. **S**   b. **A**   c. **D**
   2. a. **D**   b. **S**   c. **A**
   3. a. **A**   b. **S**   c. **D**
   4. a. **S**   b. **D**   c. **A**
   5. a. **D**   b. **A**   c. **S**

3 Fire on the High Seas
A. Finding the Main Idea
   1. **B**   2. **M**   3. **N**
B. Recalling Facts
   1. **c**   2. **b**   3. **c**   4. **b**   5. **a**
C. Making Inferences
   1. **F**   2. **C**   3. **F**   4. **C**   5. **C**
D. Using Words Precisely
   1. a. **A**   b. **S**   c. **D**
   2. a. **S**   b. **D**   c. **A**
   3. a. **A**   b. **D**   c. **S**
   4. a. **D**   b. **S**   c. **A**
   5. a. **D**   b. **S**   c. **A**

4 Pompeii: The City That Slept for 1,500 Years
A. Finding the Main Idea
   1. **B**   2. **N**   3. **M**
B. Recalling Facts
   1. **c**   2. **c**   3. **c**   4. **a**   5. **a**
C. Making Inferences
   1. **C**   2. **C**   3. **F**   4. **F**   5. **C**
D. Using Words Precisely
   1. a. **A**   b. **S**   c. **D**
   2. a. **D**   b. **S**   c. **A**
   3. a. **A**   b. **D**   c. **S**
   4. a. **S**   b. **A**   c. **D**
   5. a. **D**   b. **A**   c. **S**

5 London Falls to Ashes
A. Finding the Main Idea
   1. **N**   2. **B**   3. **M**
B. Recalling Facts
   1. **c**   2. **c**   3. **b**   4. **a**   5. **b**
C. Making Inferences
   1. **C**   2. **C**   3. **F**   4. **F**   5. **F**
D. Using Words Precisely
   1. a. **A**   b. **S**   c. **D**
   2. a. **S**   b. **A**   c. **D**
   3. a. **S**   b. **D**   c. **A**
   4. a. **A**   b. **D**   c. **S**
   5. a. **S**   b. **A**   c. **D**

6 *Hindenburg:* Last of the Great Dirigibles
A. Finding the Main Idea
   1. **M**   2. **B**   3. **N**
B. Recalling Facts
   1. **b**   2. **b**   3. **c**   4. **b**   5. **a**
C. Making Inferences
   1. **F**   2. **C**   3. **C**   4. **F**   5. **F**
D. Using Words Precisely
   1. a. **A**   b. **S**   c. **D**
   2. a. **D**   b. **A**   c. **S**
   3. a. **D**   b. **S**   c. **A**
   4. a. **S**   b. **A**   c. **D**
   5. a. **D**   b. **S**   c. **A**

7 Take to the Hills! The Johnstown Dam Is Going!
A. Finding the Main Idea
   1. **N**   2. **B**   3. **M**
B. Recalling Facts
   1. **b**   2. **b**   3. **c**   4. **a**   5. **a**
C. Making Inferences
   1. **C**   2. **C**   3. **F**   4. **C**   5. **C**
D. Using Words Precisely
   1. a. **A**   b. **D**   c. **S**
   2. a. **S**   b. **D**   c. **A**
   3. a. **S**   b. **A**   c. **D**
   4. a. **D**   b. **S**   c. **A**
   5. a. **S**   b. **D**   c. **A**

8 Death of the Unsinkable *Titanic*
A. Finding the Main Idea
  1. **B**   2. **M**   3. **N**
B. Recalling Facts
  1. **a**   2. **a**   3. **c**   4. **b**   5. **b**
C. Making Inferences
  1. **C**   2. **F**   3. **F**   4. **C**   5. **C**
D. Using Words Precisely
  1. a. **A** b. **D** c. **S**
  2. a. **S** b. **D** c. **A**
  3. a. **D** b. **A** c. **S**
  4. a. **A** b. **S** c. **D**
  5. a. **S** b. **A** c. **D**

9 Arrows' Deadly Fall to Earth
A. Finding the Main Idea
  1. **N**   2. **B**   3. **M**
B. Recalling Facts
  1. **b**   2. **c**   3. **a**   4. **a**   5. **c**
C. Making Inferences
  1. **C**   2. **F**   3. **F**   4. **F**   5. **C**
D. Using Words Precisely
  1. a. **S** b. **D** c. **A**
  2. a. **A** b. **S** c. **D**
  3. a. **D** b. **S** c. **A**
  4. a. **D** b. **A** c. **S**
  5. a. **S** b. **A** c. **D**

10 Boston's Cocoanut Grove Ablaze
A. Finding the Main Idea
  1. **B**   2. **N**   3. **M**
B. Recalling Facts
  1. **a**   2. **c**   3. **b**   4. **b**   5. **a**
C. Making Inferences
  1. **F**   2. **C**   3. **C**   4. **C**   5. **F**
D. Using Words Precisely
  1. a. **A** b. **S** c. **D**
  2. a. **S** b. **A** c. **D**
  3. a. **A** b. **S** c. **D**
  4. a. **D** b. **A** c. **S**
  5. a. **S** b. **D** c. **A**

11 Krakatoa: The Doomsday Crack Heard 'Round the World
A. Finding the Main Idea
  1. **M**   2. **B**   3. **N**
B. Recalling Facts
  1. **b**   2. **b**   3. **c**   4. **a**   5. **b**
C. Making Inferences
  1. **F**   2. **F**   3. **C**   4. **C**   5. **F**
D. Using Words Precisely
  1. a. **A** b. **S** c. **D**
  2. a. **S** b. **A** c. **D**
  3. a. **A** b. **D** c. **S**
  4. a. **A** b. **S** c. **D**
  5. a. **D** b. **S** c. **A**

12 Halifax: City Blown to Pieces
A. Finding the Main Idea
  1. **B**   2. **M**   3. **N**
B. Recalling Facts
  1. **a**   2. **b**   3. **a**   4. **b**   5. **c**
C. Making Inferences
  1. **C**   2. **C**   3. **F**   4. **C**   5. **F**
D. Using Words Precisely
  1. a. **S** b. **A** c. **D**
  2. a. **A** b. **S** c. **D**
  3. a. **S** b. **A** c. **D**
  4. a. **D** b. **A** c. **S**
  5. a. **S** b. **D** c. **A**

13 The Heroes of HMS *Birkenhead*
A. Finding the Main Idea
  1. **N**   2. **M**   3. **B**
B. Recalling Facts
  1. **a**   2. **c**   3. **a**   4. **b**   5. **a**
C. Making Inferences
  1. **F**   2. **C**   3. **C**   4. **F**   5. **F**
D. Using Words Precisely
  1. a. **S** b. **A** c. **D**
  2. a. **A** b. **S** c. **D**
  3. a. **D** b. **A** c. **S**
  4. a. **S** b. **D** c. **A**
  5. a. **A** b. **D** c. **S**

14 The Circus Troupe's Last Performance
A. Finding the Main Idea
  1. **B**   2. **N**   3. **M**
B. Recalling Facts
  1. **b**   2. **b**   3. **c**   4. **b**   5. **c**
C. Making Inferences
  1. **F**   2. **C**   3. **C**   4. **C**   5. **C**
D. Using Words Precisely
  1. a. **S** b. **A** c. **D**
  2. a. **S** b. **D** c. **A**
  3. a. **D** b. **S** c. **A**
  4. a. **A** b. **S** c. **D**
  5. a. **A** b. **S** c. **D**

15 Black Death: The End of the World
A. Finding the Main Idea
  1. **B**   2. **M**   3. **N**
B. Recalling Facts
  1. **b**   2. **a**   3. **b**   4. **b**   5. **a**
C. Making Inferences
  1. **C**   2. **F**   3. **F**   4. **C**   5. **C**
D. Using Words Precisely
  1. a. **A**   b. **D**   c. **S**
  2. a. **S**   b. **D**   c. **A**
  3. a. **S**   b. **D**   c. **A**
  4. a. **D**   b. **S**   c. **A**
  5. a. **S**   b. **A**   c. **D**

16 The Great Chicago Fire
A. Finding the Main Idea
  1. **M**   2. **N**   3. **B**
B. Recalling Facts
  1. **b**   2. **c**   3. **c**   4. **b**   5. **b**
C. Making Inferences
  1. **C**   2. **C**   3. **F**   4. **C**   5. **C**
D. Using Words Precisely
  1. a. **S**   b. **A**   c. **D**
  2. a. **A**   b. **S**   c. **D**
  3. a. **S**   b. **A**   c. **D**
  4. a. **D**   b. **S**   c. **A**
  5. a. **S**   b. **D**   c. **A**

17 The Sinking of the *Lusitania*
A. Finding the Main Idea
  1. **N**   2. **B**   3. **M**
B. Recalling Facts
  1. **c**   2. **b**   3. **a**   4. **b**   5. **a**
C. Making Inferences
  1. **C**   2. **F**   3. **F**   4. **C**   5. **C**
D. Using Words Precisely
  1. a. **A**   b. **S**   c. **D**
  2. a. **S**   b. **A**   c. **D**
  3. a. **S**   b. **D**   c. **A**
  4. a. **A**   b. **S**   c. **D**
  5. a. **A**   b. **D**   c. **S**

18 Penny-Pinching Brings Death at the World's Richest School
A. Finding the Main Idea
  1. **M**   2. **B**   3. **N**
B. Recalling Facts
  1. **b**   2. **a**   3. **c**   4. **b**   5. **a**
C. Making Inferences
  1. **F**   2. **F**   3. **C**   4. **C**   5. **C**
D. Using Words Precisely
  1. a. **A**   b. **D**   c. **S**
  2. a. **S**   b. **A**   c. **D**
  3. a. **S**   b. **D**   c. **A**
  4. a. **S**   b. **A**   c. **D**
  5. a. **D**   b. **S**   c. **A**

19 Atomic Meltdown at Chernobyl
A. Finding the Main Idea
  1. **B**   2. **M**   3. **N**
B. Recalling Facts
  1. **b**   2. **b**   3. **b**   4. **a**   5. **c**
C. Making Inferences
  1. **F**   2. **F**   3. **C**   4. **F**   5. **F**
D. Using Words Precisely
  1. a. **D**   b. **S**   c. **A**
  2. a. **A**   b. **D**   c. **S**
  3. a. **A**   b. **S**   c. **D**
  4. a. **S**   b. **A**   c. **D**
  5. a. **S**   b. **A**   c. **D**

20 The San Francisco Earthquake
A. Finding the Main Idea
  1. **B**   2. **N**   3. **M**
B. Recalling Facts
  1. **b**   2. **b**   3. **a**   4. **c**   5. **b**
C. Making Inferences
  1. **C**   2. **C**   3. **F**   4. **C**   5. **F**
D. Using Words Precisely
  1. a. **D**   b. **A**   c. **S**
  2. a. **A**   b. **S**   c. **D**
  3. a. **S**   b. **D**   c. **A**
  4. a. **D**   b. **S**   c. **A**
  5. a. **S**   b. **A**   c. **D**

21 Boston's Great Molasses Flood
A. Finding the Main Idea
  1. **B**   2. **M**   3. **N**
B. Recalling Facts
  1. **b**   2. **c**   3. **c**   4. **a**   5. **c**
C. Making Inferences
  1. **F**   2. **F**   3. **F**   4. **F**   5. **C**
D. Using Words Precisely
  1. a. **A**   b. **S**   c. **D**
  2. a. **D**   b. **A**   c. **S**
  3. a. **A**   b. **D**   c. **S**
  4. a. **S**   b. **A**   c. **D**
  5. a. **S**   b. **D**   c. **A**

WORDS-PER-MINUTE TABLE
& PROGRESS GRAPHS

Words per Minute

Unit ▶	Sample	1	2	3	4	5	6	7	
No. of Words ▶	1103	1103	1130	1023	838	1101	927	1139	
1:30	735	735	753	682	558	734	618	759	90
1:40	664	664	680	616	504	663	558	686	100
1:50	602	602	617	559	457	601	506	622	110
2:00	551	551	565	511	419	550	463	569	120
2:10	510	510	523	473	387	509	429	527	130
2:20	473	473	485	439	359	472	397	488	140
2:30	441	441	452	409	335	440	370	455	150
2:40	414	414	424	384	315	414	348	428	160
2:50	389	389	399	361	296	389	327	402	170
3:00	367	367	376	341	279	367	309	379	180
3:10	349	349	357	323	265	348	293	360	190
3:20	331	331	339	307	251	330	278	342	200
3:30	315	315	322	292	239	314	264	325	210
3:40	301	301	308	279	228	300	253	311	220
3:50	287	287	295	267	218	287	242	297	230
4:00	275	275	282	255	209	275	231	284	240
4:10	265	265	271	246	201	264	222	273	250
4:20	254	254	261	236	193	254	214	263	260
4:30	245	245	251	227	186	244	206	253	270
4:40	236	236	242	219	179	236	198	244	280
4:50	228	228	234	211	173	228	191	235	290
5:00	220	220	226	204	167	220	185	227	300
5:10	213	213	219	198	162	213	179	220	310
5:20	206	206	212	192	157	206	173	213	320
5:30	200	200	205	186	152	200	168	207	330
5:40	194	194	199	180	148	194	163	201	340
5:50	189	189	194	175	143	188	159	195	350
6:00	183	183	188	170	139	183	154	190	360
6:10	179	179	183	166	136	178	150	184	370
6:20	174	174	178	161	132	174	146	180	380
6:30	169	169	174	157	128	169	142	175	390
6:40	165	165	169	153	125	165	139	171	400
6:50	161	161	165	149	122	161	135	166	410
7:00	157	157	161	146	119	157	132	162	420
7:20	150	150	154	139	114	150	126	155	440
7:40	143	143	147	133	109	143	121	148	460
8:00	137	137	141	127	104	137	115	142	480

Minutes and Seconds ▶ (left axis) — *Seconds* ◀ (right axis)